The Canine Library

The
Staffordshire
Bull Terrier

The

Staffordshire
Bull Terrier

W. M. MORLEY

Beech Publishing House
Station Yard
Elsted Marsh
MIDHURST
West Sussex GU29 0JT

ISBN 1-85736-256-X
First published 1982
Reprinted 1982, 1983 & 1984
Second Edition 2004

British Library Cataloguing-in-Publication Data
A catalogue record for this book is available
from the British Library.

Printed and bound by Antony Rowe Ltd, Eastbourne

Beech Publishing House
Station Yard
Elsted Marsh
MIDHURST
West Sussex   GU29   0JT

CONTENTS

APPENDICES

FOREWORD

Although my canine interests encompass many breeds and my judging activities are now international, I have for so long been an admirer of the Staffordshire Bull Terrier that it gives me great pleasure to write a preface to this new book on the breed.

Staffords, with their short coats and their undoubted affection for their human friends, make ideal companions; it is not surprising, therefore, that they are now the third most popular breed of terriers and promise to improve their position still further.

I first met the author over thirty years ago when I came to work and live in the north-east. He and his wife owned some very fine Staffords at that time and were fortunate enough to breed the first North Eastern Champion in the breed. Mr Morley's professional work restricted his leisure activities for some years, but he retained his interest in the breed and over a long period has accumulated a great deal of experience, which he has now condensed into this book.

As an educationalist he has had ample opportunity to manipulate words, and the result is a book which will appeal to all interested in the breed whether they be novices or seasoned campaigners. In my view this is a most useful reference book, which will be of value for many years to come.

Reg Gadsden
Vice Chairman
Kennel Club Liaison Council

ACKNOWLEDGEMENTS

No man is an island and few authors can write a book of this nature without a little help from their friends. Such assistance has been generously given by many Staffordshire Bull Terrier enthusiasts from all parts of the country and from overseas.

I would particularly thank Gordon Clark of Newcastle-upon-Tyne for providing photographs of early Bulldogs and Bull and Terriers, and Mike Homan of London for additional information on the early sporting history of the breed.

Gratitude is also extended to my old friend Ronnie Stevens for the line drawings and to the many owners of Staffordshire Bull Terriers who generously supplied photographs. It is regretted that, owing to limitations of space, it has been impossible to include all these.

When so many enthusiasts have co-operated I hope it is not invidious to mention specifically Bill Boylan, one of the original members of the Staffordshire Bull Terrier Club now living in retirement in Suffolk; Gerald Dudley, owner of the famous Wychbury Kennels; Ken Bailey whose late Ch Benext Beau still holds the record for the greatest number of challenge certificates in the breed; Eddie Pringle, Chairman of the Breed Council, and his wife Mary, breed correspondent of *Dog World*.

Members of other breed clubs have also supplied information: Jim Parsons, Tom Fletcher and Alan Mitchell from Wales and the South West; Dr A. Anderson, Ian and Jessie Dunn and Jean Short from Scotland; June Fisher, Ken Fensom and Alec Waters from the South; David and June Horsfall, Norman Berry and Les Aspin from the North West; and Malcolm Boam and John Monks from the Midlands; the list is by no means exhaustive.

Nearer home, members of the North Eastern Club have given their assistance, particularly Jack Miller of Rellim fame; Ken and Maureen Brown of the Moekens Kennels; Tom Spashett, Jack Dunn, Glynn Carter, Les Winward, and my wife, who has encouraged and supported me in this venture.

Finally I wish to thank my publishers for their assistance in presenting the manuscript, the Kennel Club for allowing me to reproduce extracts from their regulations and official documents, and its officers for their kind co-operation.

INTRODUCTION

The main factor that prompted me to write this book was the opportunity to combine two of my principal hobbies: the Staffordshire Bull Terrier and writing.

Since we acquired our first Stafford in 1948, my wife and I have increasingly admired both the physical and mental characteristics of the breed, which we believe to be superior to those of any other breed of dog. During the past thirty years there has been a tremendous increase in the popularity of the Staffordshire Bull Terrier as more people have become aware of the pleasures of owning specimens of the breed.

Although a considerable number of owners exhibit their Staffords — and undoubtedly the show-ring is a prerequisite for the continuing popularity of any breed of dog — there are many owners who, for a variety of reasons, are not so interested in showing their dogs. Nevertheless, they may have an important contribution to make to the future of this breed, and many are interested in obtaining as much information as possible in order to be better informed about their hobby.

This book has been designed, therefore, to be of interest to a wide range of Stafford owners, from beginners in the breed to experienced breeders and exhibitors. It is hoped that the contents may also prove of value to owners of other breeds of dogs, especially other sporting breeds, who are not yet fully conversant with the peculiarities and propensities of the Staffordshire Bull Terrier.

PUBLISHERS' FOREWORD

We have great pleasure in republishing the late Mr Morley's book on the Staffordshire Bull Terrier. My wife and I kept the breed for many years and found that they were outstanding dogs in terms of loyalty and affection. In fact, when we lived in Scotland we were quite near to Dr A Anderson who was one of the pioneers of the breed and we often visited her and kept dogs from her Bourtie Kennel.

Times have changed, but even in the 1980s there were those who criticized the book on the grounds of alleged promotion of the fighting dog. Yet all the author was stating, at times quite enthusiastically, that the breed was developed from the original fighting dog. Today the KC standard states that the breed is "Traditionally of indomitable courage and tenacity". Mr Morley was therefore giving due emphasis to the true nature of the breed.

With the *Dangerous Dogs Act* those who wish to keep Staffordshires must try to adhere to the standards and not keep dogs which do not comply with the true to breed characteristics. Those which are tall or excessively muscular and without pedigree might be frowned upon by the Courts who have a duty to decide whether a dog is dangerous and should be destroyed. Keeping breeding records and registering with the Kennel Club might provide a defence against any action taken on the grounds of appearance alone.

Our thanks go to those who assisted. Mrs Jean Loughborough, Mr and Mrs Stanway, Mr T Spashett and others gave assistance. The Kennel Club provided an up to date list of Champions.

The list of secretaries of the local breed clubs has been omitted because this information quickly becomes out of date and can, in any case, be obtained from the Kennel Club. This also applies to the number of dogs registered.

Joseph Batty   *Elsted Marsh,   May, 2004*

CH. ELVINOR PIED PRINCESS AT WAYSTAFF
Bred: Mr & Mrs Emett. Owners: Mr & Mrs Stanway

CH. CRASHKON MEL BEE
Bred by Mrs L Williams
Owned jointly by Mr and Mrs Stanway and Mr and
Mrs Albutt

1
CHARACTER AND TEMPERAMENT

It is probable that most Stafford owners were originally attracted to the breed by the marvellous temperament of the dogs; I certainly was.

Although there are inevitably individual temperamental differences, most Staffords appear to portray certain characteristics that are typical of the breed, including a great affection for their human friends, an ability to adapt readily to widely different environments and an apparent imperviousness to pain.

These virtues, together with the Stafford's undoubted courage, intelligence, fearlessness and tenacity, make it a particularly attractive dog to possess, and it is not surprising that Kennel Club registrations have increased to such an extent that Staffordshire Bull Terriers are now the most popular breed of terrier having overhauled West Highland White Terriers and Cairn Terriers, the only terrier breeds previously placed above Staffords in the Kennel Club 'league table'.

Another somewhat less objective view, formed after keeping Staffordshire Bull Terriers for many years, is that they possess an indefinable temperamental quality, which can be described only as some form of 'humanisation'.

Of course, the character and temperament of any dog, and indeed all behaviour, depend on various combinations of heredity and environment. In over-simplified canine terms the critical factors can be said to be breeding, upbringing and training. Most Staffords are particularly friendly to all humans, few in my experience possessing unreliable tempers, and because of this, I tend to disagree with those who claim that Staffords are naturally good guard dogs. Indeed, if one keeps a number of dogs and no specific training is given, Staffords are not usually good guards of property, as they are much too well disposed towards human predators. There are, of course, exceptions, including many dogs kept individually as family pets; no doubt with training such dogs could become quite good property guards. A number of Staffords kept together can also be trained as guards and will certainly give warning of any unnatural sounds or movements, but, unless they are trained for the task, they will not normally attack humans.

A notable exception to this is the number of Staffords that spend a great deal of time in their owners' cars. Probably because they come to regard the confined interior of the vehicle as their private domain, they quickly acquire a sense of possessiveness which deters intruders. I have known the most tractable Stafford acquire what appears to be a completely different character if anyone tries to enter the car during the owner's absence. I am not quite sure why this should be so; it may be that in the comparatively small interior of a car possibly filled with its owner's personal belongings, the Stafford assumes the role of *personal* guard rather than a guard of property.

Staffords as personal guards are an entirely different proposition. The individual house pet generally needs no training in this respect, especially as the association with his master or mistress progresses and a sound relationship is formed. The Stafford excels as an undemanding companion, a selfless personal guard and a peerless car attendant.

It is well known that although certain strains may differ, the average Stafford does not reach full physical maturity until at least two years old, and owners should be careful of condemning their dogs for an apparent lack of spirit until they reach full maturity. Many examples of the breed have shown little so-called spirit in their formative stages, but, on maturity, have astonished their owners, not to mention many other quadrupeds.

I recall one stud dog we owned, which, although well balanced, was taller and heavier than the present Standard allows. He was approaching two years of age, and, as our other Staffords were all bitches, he had never had occasion to be anything other than boisterously playful. One day Prince was attacked by a large cross-bred Irish Wolfhound weighing probably 100lb, which was regarded as the canine scourge of the neighbourhood. The mongrel charged forward, and I stared incredulously as Prince lay flat on his belly; for a fearful moment I thought I had nurtured a dog that was not a true Stafford. I need not have worried; as soon as the mongrel came within a few feet, Prince suddenly pounced, sinking his huge teeth into his opponent's cheek and jaw. Within seconds the mongrel was screaming for its life, and it took considerable effort to disengage the dogs, after which the mongrel ignominiously retreated. Not surprisingly, the owner of that dog has not spoken to me since! Even Dale Carnegie may have agreed that it is not so easy to 'win friends and influence people' – especially if you own a fighting Stafford!

For those who have yet to purchase a Stafford, but are contemplating doing so, it must be remembered that Staffords are historically fighting dogs and that unless they are kept tightly under control there is always a possibility that they will fight.

Of course, individual specimens differ greatly. There are those that constantly appear to want to fight anything within reach; contrary to popular belief, not all such dogs lack the true Stafford temperament, although I have known some that do. Ideally, all Stafford owners would like to possess specimens of the breed that are normally quiet, well behaved animals, and that respond only when provoked; alas, we do not live in such a perfect world.

Newcomers to the breed may at first be somewhat bewildered by the apparently conflicting comments that they read and hear, and they may be forgiven for thinking that the 'temperament' of their dogs ranges from that of some insane devil intent upon genocide, to that of a whimpering lap-dog avoiding confrontation at all costs. Of course, as is usual in these circumstances, the truth probably lies somewhere between these extremes. It must also be recognised that there are individual variations within the breed – and there always have been! However, the vast majority of Staffords fit into a much narrower spectrum of behaviour patterns. These patterns may be difficult to define, but the much maligned Standard provides a useful guide in defining the characteristics of the breed: 'indomitable courage, high intelligence, tenacity . . . affection for his friends and children in particular ... off-duty quietness and trustworthy stability.'

Over recent years a great deal of controversy has surrounded the supposed aggressiveness of Staffords. If aggressive is defined simply as meaning 'ready to attack' or 'forceful', then surely Staffords should possess this characteristic; if it means 'provoking a quarrel' or 'exhibiting offensive behaviour' then there may be room for debate.

Perhaps it is as difficult to generalise about canine behaviour as it is to generalise about human behaviour. Humans who frequently exhibit aggressive symptoms are not always too courageous in combat – but there are exceptions! So it is with dogs. Ideally, most of us would prefer our Staffords to act as 'perfect gentlemen' until provoked and then to react with the courage and tenacity that should be inherent. Many of us have been fortunate to possess dogs of this type, and I believe this to be a feature of the 'true' Stafford temperament; some of us however have owned at least one dog which betrayed somewhat different characteristics.

Paradoxically, the Stafford which is supposedly full of fire may not be exhibiting the true traits of the breed; in my experience the real fighting dogs I have owned have been friendly animals, friendly even to other dogs – until provocation time. Again there are exceptions!

I recall attending a championship show many years ago when a real fighting machine was being exhibited, a dog that, unfortunately, appeared completely lethargic while in the show-ring. In some ways he was an enigma, as owners of other dogs, who were not familiar with him, assumed that he was somewhat timid, despite his size. He was placed alongside a snarling dog, which was straining at the leash and was uncontrolled by his handler, who appeared to be enjoying the spectacle of his charge challenging all and sundry within the ring. Momentarily the handler became distracted, and immediately his charge released himself and attacked his nearest neighbour. Within seconds the jaws of 'old softy' were firmly embedded in the aggressor's throat, and eventually the unfortunate animal had to be withdrawn from the show, much the worse for wear. The story may not be typical, but it is possibly worth thinking about.

Although I have kept Staffordshire Bull Terriers for over thirty years, I cannot honestly say that in recent years I have noticed a marked *percentage* increase in temperamentally unsound dogs; there may be more such animals existing today, but there are, of course, many more Staffords! Most specimens of the breed continue to display the desirable facets of character well defined in the Standard. True, we may not now possess the same number of dynamic fighting machines that we did thirty years ago, but there are physical as well as temperamental reasons for this. At the same time it must be recognised that a minority of champions of that era would not have been able to have given good accounts of themselves in a real dog fight.

I should conclude by stating that breeders should be completely ruthless in discarding temperamentally unsound stock from their breeding programmes. This seems essential, as it is in this area that the real charm and attraction of the breed lies; the physical appearance of the Stafford, while of supreme importance in the show-ring, pales into insignificance compared with its character. We can, perhaps with some difficulty, assess the relative physical attribute of a Stafford by reference to the Breed Standard; it would take a very rash individual indeed to claim that the temperament of an individual dog could be so easily determined.

2
EARLY ANCESTRY

Although it is possible to trace the early history of dogs – if somewhat tenuously – from about 3000 BC, the further we go back into time, the less accurate our information.

Some type of dog has presumably been kept by the human race since earliest times, but the Romans made the first recorded attempt to classify their dogs into categories which make sense even today. The three groups were all entirely functional – hunting dogs, shepherding dogs and watch dogs. It was probably much later when an official sporting group appeared, although no doubt dogs were used even at this time for some types of sporting activity.

Early Britain was supposed to be famed for a large breed known as a 'mastyve' of 'mastiff', which appears to have been an indigenous breed, although some records indicate that the Bulldog existed at that time. Whether or not they were variations of the same breed is difficult to determine. Certainly Bulldogs, or 'Butchers' Dogs' as they were sometimes known, existed during the twelfth century and were used for bull baiting, a sport which continued for over six hundred years. Many changes occurred during this period, and the original large, mastiff-type animal, which was used to fight against an untethered bull, was replaced by a lighter dog, which attacked tethered bulls and relied on agility, as well as strength, to accomplish his task.

The term 'terrier' appears to have been used somewhat generically to identify any smaller breed of dog that may have been used for a variety of purposes. It is against this somewhat ragged backcloth that we must endeavour to trace the early history of the Staffordshire Bull Terrier.

Minor disagreements still abound, but it is generally accepted that the modern Staffordshire Bull Terrier is a direct descendant of dogs of mixed origin, generally known during most of the nineteenth and the early twentieth centuries, as the Bull and Terrier.

Writers on the breed have suggested that this original cross-breeding may have taken place about 1800, but the facts are uncertain, and it is possible that similar types of dog appeared before this date. It has also been stated that the Bull and Terrier of the early nineteenth century derived from the Bulldog of that time and the Old English Terrier in an attempt to produce a fighting dog with the strength of the former and the agility of the latter. Some credence can be attached to this theory as it was about this period that the sports of bear baiting and bull baiting (finally made illegal in 1835) began to decline, to be superseded by organised dog fighting.

It is probable, however, that our pragmatic forefathers used the most successful fighting dogs, whatever their pedigrees, as the sires and dams in their breeding programmes; success at fighting was the main criterion. It is fairly safe to assume that early breeders were not so influenced by the 'looks or books' theory as by the performance of their dogs in the dog pits. But the Bulldog of that era (not to be confused with the modern species of that name) and any game terrier type of dog showing agility and tenacity probably formed the basis of the present Staffordshire Bull Terrier.

The fighting dog, like his human counterpart the prize fighter, required strength, agility, skill and the capacity to both give and receive severe punishment. Today, strength and agility are the main physical characteristics of the breed, and many of our most temperamentally sound dogs seem completely impervious even to extremes of pain.

In the latter part of the nineteenth century, pedigree dog breeding began to be taken more seriously, and the Bull and Terrier, or Pit Dog as it was sometimes called, achieved a certain amount of notoriety because of its somewhat unpalatable past. It was because of the enthusiasm and dedication of the miners and ironworkers that the breed was preserved, and it was fitting that the Staffordshire Bull Terrier Club found its beginnings in Cradley Heath.

Towards the end of 1934, a number of enthusiasts discussed at a series of informal meetings, the possible formation of a breed club, but this was not officially established until May 1935. Over forty breeders attended a meeting at the Old Cross Guns Hotel, Cradley Heath, where Joe Mallen, later to make quite a name in the breed, was the landlord. Although the majority of those present opted for the title 'The Original Staffordshire Bull Terrier Club', this found little favour with the Kennel Club, and the registered name became simply 'The Staffordshire Bull Terrier Club'. Possibly the word 'original' reflected a desire to record that this breed was more directly descended from the original Bull and Terrier than was the Bull Terrier, which had been recognised as a breed by the Kennel Club some years previously.

The 'White' Bull and Terrier originated by James Hinks of Birmingham about the middle of the nineteenth century, was an amalgam of a number of breeds; even today many different theories exist relating to its origins. Certainly the down face, which typifies the breed, is not found in many other dogs; the Collie and the Bedlington Terrier have it, and it has been suggested that the 'White Collie' made a significant contribution to the evolution of the Bull Terrier – also down faced. Theories have been advanced that Dalmatian blood was also used, although it is only recently that the Bedlington Terrier has been mentioned as a possible contributor! Whatever its origins, the breed quickly gained popularity.

At the risk of stating the obvious, the Bull Terrier differs significantly from the Staffordshire Bull Terrier both physically and mentally. While neither height nor weight limits are specified for the Bull Terrier, the breed is generally taller and heavier than the Stafford. The heads are completely different; the Stafford has a distinct stop between the skull and muzzle; the Bull Terrier is down faced. The Stafford has round eyes set to look ahead and rose ears; the Bull Terrier's eyes are placed obliquely, are triangular and deep-set, and it has prick ears.

Bull Terrier enthusiasts tell us that their breed's type of eye is preferable in a fighting dog and that the Bull Terrier's head is more suitable for fighting. I doubt it. Although, in theory, the eye of the Stafford may appear more vulnerable, the general head conformation, with its broad skull and pronounced cheek muscles, make it a harder-biting dog; it also has greater agility and tenacity.

During the early part of the twentieth century there certainly appears to have been a great deal of crossing of the two breeds, and photographs of this period show numerous specimens which seem to have Stafford bodies and Bull Terrier heads. This is one of the reasons why even today we produce the occasional Stafford noticeably lacking the necessary 'stop' between skull and muzzle.

The Staffordshire Bull Terrier Club's first officers were two breeders who were later to influence the progress of not only the club, but also the breed; Jack Barnard was elected president and Joe Dunn became secretary. Jack Barnard (whom I replaced as Staffordshire Bull Terrier contributor to the now defunct *Dog Fancier* when he decided to retire) divided his canine interests between Staffords and Bull Mastiffs and was always willing to share with me his firsthand knowledge of the early days of the breed. Although not universally acknowledged, Jack Barnard affirmed that it was his dog Jim the Dandy which became the blueprint from which the first Breed Standard derived. At this time Jim the Dandy was a mature dog, nearly three years old, standing $17\frac{1}{2}$in at the shoulder and weighing 33lb. The circumference of his skull was 17in, which is relatively small compared with today's dogs; indeed, not only was the original Standard amended in 1948 but a different type of dog has evolved in the forty-six years since the Club was originally formed.

3
DEVELOPMENT OF THE BREED

1935–48

Despite early enthusiasm, the progress of registered stock was somewhat slow. Kennel Club Registrations rose from 174 in 1935 to 310 in 1939, a modest increase, halted only temporarily by the outbreak of war in 1939, for 360 Staffords were registered in 1942, rising to a total of 1097 by the end of 1945. After the war the increasing popularity of the breed became apparent, and in 1949, the year when the Standard was finally altered, registrations rose to 2357.

Although the 'Bull and Terrier' had existed for over a hundred years, its appearance had been considered much less important than its performance; certainly there had been little attempt at standardisation. A great deal of variation existed between specimens of Staffordshire Bull Terrier, and it was against this backcloth that the Staffordshire Bull Terrier Club was required to formulate a Standard. The result was the following Standard, which survived until 1949, when it was altered only slightly – but some think importantly – to what it is today.

1935 Breed Standard

General appearance   The Staffordshire Bull Terrier is a smooth-coated dog, standing about 15 to 18in high at the shoulder. He should give the impression of great strength for his size, and, although muscular, should be active and agile.

Head   Short, deep through, broad skull, very pronounced cheek muscles, distinct stop, short foreface, mouth level.

Ears   Rose, half prick and prick; these three to be preferred, full drop to be penalized.

Eyes   Dark.

Neck   Should be muscular and rather short.

Body   Short back, deep brisket, light in loins with forelegs set rather wide apart to permit chest development.

Front legs   Straight, feet well padded, to turn out a little and showing no weakness at pasterns.
Hind legs   Hindquarters well muscled, let down at hocks like a terrier.
Coat   Short, smooth and close to skin.
Tail   The tail should be of medium length tapering to a point and carried rather low; it should not curl much and may be compared with an old fashioned pump handle.
Weight   Dogs 28 to 38lb. Bitches 4lb less.
Colour   May be any shade of brindle, black, white, fawn or red, or any of these colours with white. Black-and-tan and liver not to be encouraged.
Faults to be penalised   Dudley nose, light or pink eyes (rims), tail too long or badly curled, badly undershot or overshot mouths.

Scale of Points

General appearance, coat and condition	15
Head	30
Neck	10
Body	25
Legs and Feet	15
Tail	5
	100

Despite the attempts at flexibility in the Standard, it is interesting to note that a scale of points was attached, presumably to help judges assess specimens of the breed. It would have been difficult to have formulated a Standard that found general favour and certainly the introduction of a scale of points must have been contentious in the extreme, even if it was to be used in conjunction with the Standard.

The Staffordshire Bull Terrier Club's first show was an outdoor event held at Cradley Heath on 17 August 1935, with H. N. Beilby as judge. Not surprisingly perhaps, the leading dog, from an entry of over sixty exhibits, was Jim the Dandy and second in the Open Dog class was Game Lad, founder of the 'L' line (see p 112); the Open Bitch class was won by Brave Nell, with Queenie second.

This show was not in fact the first to schedule classes for Staffords. On 11 June 1935, the Hertfordshire Agricultural

Society, no doubt prompted by Bill Boylan, a Bilston-based founder-member of the Staffordshire Bull Terrier Club then living in St Albans, included two Stafford classes in its Open Show held in Hatfield Park. The judge, Sam Crabtree, an all-rounder of the period, made Game Lad best Stafford, despite strong competition from dogs owned by the well-known comedy actor Tom Walls.

Probably the next important landmark in the show history of the breed was Crufts 1936 – the first time Staffords had been included at this prestigious event. Joe Dunn was appointed judge and made Joe Mallen's Cross Guns Johnson best of breed.

Three other breed clubs were formed during this period. The Southern Counties Staffordshire Bull Terrier Society, formed in 1937, had Tom Walls as its first president. The Northern Counties Staffordshire Bull Terrier Club commenced operations in 1943, and the North West Staffordshire Bull Terrier Club, with its activities centred around Manchester, in 1946.

Perhaps fittingly, the Birmingham National Show provided the venue for the first challenge certificates to be awarded to Staffordshire Bull Terriers. This was at the 1938 Championship Show, when A. Demaine, a member of the first Staffordshire Bull Terrier Club, awarded the dog challenge certificate to H. Boxley's Vindictive Montyson and the bitch challenge certificate to Joe Dunn's Lady Eve.

Championship shows followed at Crufts, Cheltenham and Bath, and it was at Bath on 4 May 1939 that the first champions of the breed were crowned; A. W. Fulwood awarded the dog challenge certificate to Champion Gentleman Jim and the bitch challenge certificate to Champion Lady Eve.

The first post-war championship show, organised by the Southern Counties Staffordshire Bull Terrier Society, was held in June 1946, with nearly three hundred entries. Not until August 1946 did the parent body, the Staffordshire Bull Terrier Club, hold its first championship show. At this event in the Coventry Drill Hall, Dan Potter and Fred Holden, the duo who frequently worked together, were the judges, and the show attracted approximately three hundred entries.

In the thirteen years between the breed's acceptance by the

Kennel Club in 1935 and the formulation of the new Breed Standard in 1948, registrations of new stock grew from 174 to a total of 2211. The individual years' registrations are given in Appendix 1.

Since 1948: The Present Breed Standard

It was in 1949 that the Kennel Club finally approved a new Standard which replaced the original Standard formulated by the Staffordshire Bull Terrier Club in 1935. The full and present Standard of the breed is detailed below.

Kennel Club Standard of the Staffordshire Bull Terrier

Characteristics From the past history of the Staffordshire Bull Terrier, the modern dog draws his character of indomitable courage, high intelligence and tenacity. This, coupled with his affection for his friends, and children in particular, his off-duty quietness and trustworthy stability, makes him the foremost all-purpose dog.

General appearance The Staffordshire Bull Terrier is a smooth-coated dog. He should be of great strength for his size and, although muscular, should be active and agile.

Head and skull Short, deep through, broad skull, very pronounced cheek muscles, distinct stop, short foreface, black nose.

Eyes Dark preferable but may bear some relation to coat colour. Round of medium size, and set to look straight ahead.

Ears Rose or half prick and not large. Full drop or prick to be penalised.

Mouth The mouth should be level, ie the incisors of the bottom jaw should fit closely inside the incisors of the top jaw, and the lips should be tight and clean. The badly undershot or overshot mouth to be heavily penalised.

Neck Muscular, rather short, clean in outline and gradually widening towards the shoulders.

Forequarters Legs straight and well boned, set rather wide apart, without looseness at the shoulders, and showing no weakness at the pasterns, from which point the feet turn out a little.

Body The body should be close coupled, with a level topline, wide front, deep brisket, well sprung ribs and rather light in the loins.

Hindquarters The hindquarters should be well muscled, hocks let down with stifles well bent. Legs should be parallel when viewed from behind.

Feet The feet should be well padded, strong and of medium size.

Tail   The tail should be of medium length, low set, tapering to a point and carried rather low. It should not curl and may be likened to an old fashioned pump handle.

Coat   Smooth, short, and close to the skin.

Colour   Red, fawn, white, black or blue, or any of these colours with white. Any shade of brindle or any shade of brindle with white. Black-and-tan or liver colour not to be encouraged.

Weight and size   Weight: dogs 12·7–17·24k (28–38lb); bitches 10·89–15·42k (24–34lb). Height (at shoulder): 35·56–40·64cm (14–16in), these heights being related to weight.

Faults   To be penalised in accordance with the severity of the fault: light eyes or pink eye rims. Tails too long or badly curled. Non-conformation to the limits of weight or height. Full drop or prick ears. Undershot or overshot mouths.

The following faults should debar a dog from winning any prize: Pink (Dudley) nose. Badly undershot or overshot mouth. Badly undershot: where the lower jaw protrudes to such an extent that the incisors of the lower jaw do not touch those of the upper jaw. Badly overshot: where the upper jaw protrudes to such an extent that the incisors of the upper jaw do not touch those of the lower jaw.

Note   Male animals should have two apparently normal testicles fully descended into the scrotum.

Thirty years' experience of the workings of the revised Standard and its comparison with the original one of 1935, do throw up some conclusions on the way the breed has developed.

Characteristics

This section was omitted from the original Standard. It states in broad terms the desired temperamental characteristics of the breed. How one measures these characteristics is not clear; indeed in the confines of the show-ring it is impossible. However, the temperamental attributes mentioned in the present Breed Standard are undoubtedly present in the most typical Staffords, even if – in my view – they can be determined only by a lengthy association with a particular dog. (More detailed information is included in Chapter 1).

General appearance

The original Standard decreed a height of 'about 15 to 18in at the shoulder'. The present Standard omits reference to size

'Bull Baiting' by F. Barlow, late seventeenth century. The untethered bull is being attacked by a dog of indeterminate ancestry, though with obvious bulldog characteristics

An early Bull and Terrier by Henry Alken, about 1820. The head portrays some terrier affinity, unlike the pronounced undershot jaws of bulldogs of the period

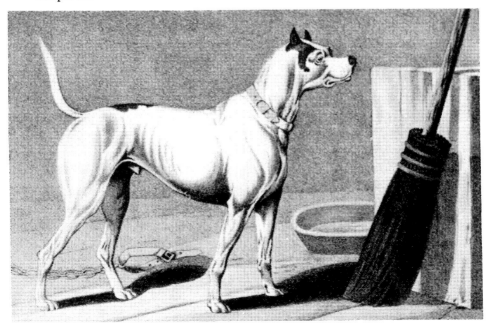

Ch Rellim A'boy, born 1957. This striking pied dog, owned and bred by Mrs Terry Miller, produced the prolific sire Ch Ferryvale Victor

Tiara of Roxette (*left*) with her daughter Georgia, both owned by Mr B. Greenyer and his son (*Panther Photographic International*)

Joe Mallen, Staffordshire iron worker, and his dog Ch Gentleman Jim, the breed's first dog champion

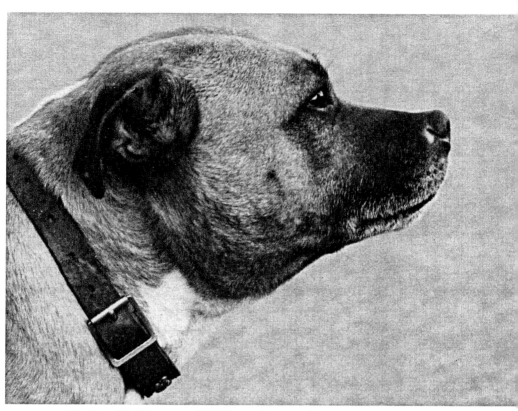

Ch Cottfol Princess of Tridwr whose well proportioned feminine head helped to win her eleven challenge certificates and ten point Green Stars

Tojen Carmen, bred by Mrs M. Briscoe out of Tojen Tomanda (*Animal Photography Ltd*)

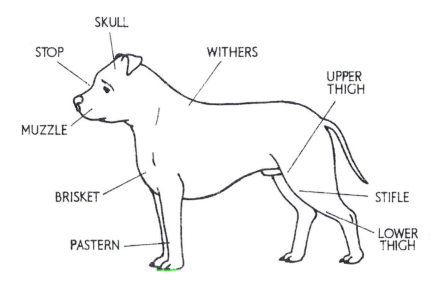

Important points in Stafford conformation

under this heading but later includes a special 'weight and size' paragraph, which is of great importance and will be dealt with under that heading. The impression of strength and agility is of supreme importance, as this combination of qualities is essential in a dog originally conceived for fighting. Some of the earlier enthusiasts aver that many of today's dogs are physically as well as temperamentally less suited for fighting than their ancestors of fifty years ago. I have no personal experience of dogs of this period, but I believe that in general they *have* retained their reputation for being the most effective canine fighting breed, truly represented by one of our Breed Club's well-chosen if not entirely original motto – *Nemo me impune lacessit* (nobody provokes me with impunity).

Exhibitors should realise that as soon as their charges enter the show-ring, many judges, perhaps subconsciously, receive immediate impressions of each individual dog; if this impression is favourable, the exhibit is generally at an advantage. An exhibit looking well balanced, with plenty of substance, possessing a glistening coat and a bright expression, is the type judges look for when selecting their short lists. Conversely, a lethargic dog, showing little interest in the judicial proceedings often fails to do justice to himself or his owner.

For some inexplicable reason, some Stafford exhibitors seem to hold the view that a barking, snarling dog, straining at the leash, ostensibly wishing to fight any or all of his opponents in the ring, is a desirable representative of the breed. They are mistaken. Certainly some such dogs may possess the correct Stafford temperament, but nevertheless they should be properly controlled in the show-ring. It does no credit to the handler when his dog pulls him from one end of the ring to the other, allowing the judge little opportunity to assess movement, from which the soundness of parts of the dog's anatomical structure can often be gauged. Good behaviour in the show-ring is something we should all aim for and, with the occasional exception, is something which can be achieved with patience and experience. It may be true that certain handlers purposely allow their dogs to rush towards the judge in an attempt to hide such defects as shoulder malformation. This is not necessarily cheating, as the best judges will undoubtedly be aware of these and other methods of ring behaviour, and react accordingly.

Head and skull

This paragraph contains the same wording in both Standards, the only difference being that in the original Standard the title of the paragraph is 'Head' and in the current Standard 'Head and Skull'. It would be difficult for a dog to have a head without a skull! In the 1935 Standard, used in conjunction with a system of points, 30 of the total 100 points were awarded for the head, and even today many judges seem to attach great importance to this aspect of Stafford anatomy. Perhaps they are right.

Although many breed enthusiasts have endeavoured over a long period to analyse good heads by measurement, it is not really such a simple issue. While the girth and the length of the skull and the muzzle, and the angle of the skull and of the muzzle are all-important, their interrelationship is of supreme importance and all must be considered when assessing any head. Even though a broad skull and a short foreface are required by the Breed Standard, there should be a well balanced appearance; a large skull requires a somewhat heavier muzzle. Further, a distinct stop between skull and muzzle is essential and the degree

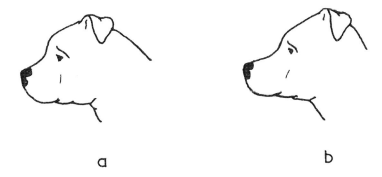

(a) Typical short, heavy muzzle; (b) less desirable larger, lighter muzzle

of the stop regulates part of the relationship between skull and muzzle. Most of the highly regarded heads show that if a line is drawn from the base of the eye parallel to the top line of the skull, and another line is drawn through the top line of the muzzle, the latter line should be slightly higher, giving an angle of between 8° and 10°; in other words a slight amount of 'dish face' is required.

Neither a completely square muzzle, which gives a 'cloddish' effect, nor a pointed muzzle, which looks somewhat 'snipey', is desirable; a *slightly* tapered muzzle is generally considered to be the most acceptable.

Ears

The original Standard allowed rose, half-pricked or pricked ears; the later Standard stipulates rose or half-pricked, with the added requirement that they should be 'not large'. In practice most of the best modern Staffords have rose ears.

It is surprising how a dog's expression is altered by the size, shape and carriage of its ears. A small, neat rose ear, which can

Typical rose ear held
in good position

be folded backwards beyond the reach of an adversary, is, of course, the ultimate aim. If the ears are carried too low they tend to contribute to a rather torpid expression; if they are carried too high, although presenting a brighter countenance, they are usually somewhat detrimental to the general balance of the head.

Eyes

Originally all eyes were to be dark, but the present Standard, although preferring dark eyes, allows them to have some relation to coat colour. Despite this, most fanciers prefer the dark eye in all their dogs although this part of the Standard should be borne in mind when exhibits are judged. It is now further stipulated that eyes must be 'round, of medium size and set to look straight ahead'. Certainly expression is dictated to some extent by the set, size, shape and colour of the eye. The distance between the eyes is of the greatest importance as even a small difference in measurement can create major differences in expression. I never cease to be amazed by judges' critiques which state that a dog 'gave me a good honest look'. It would be much more impressive to read that the judge had given the dog a good honest look!

Mouth

Mouths did not warrant a separate section in the original Standard, which did, however, specify a level mouth and decreed that badly undershot or overshot mouths were faults to be penalised under the relevant section. The current Standard defines a level mouth: 'the incisors of the bottom jaw should fit closely inside the incisors of the top jaw. The badly undershot or overshot mouth is to be heavily penalised.' It is further specified that lips, part of the anatomy not originally mentioned, should be tight and clean. Lippiness would naturally not be encouraged in a fighting dog.

Unfortunately during the past few years some 'experts' have tended to underestimate the seriousness of badly undershot jaws and have publicly stated that they would have no hesitation in using an undershot stud dog. Let us not delude ourselves. An undershot, or indeed an overshot, mouth is a serious fault in a fighting dog; a badly undershot mouth is a very serious fault indeed. Ideally we should aim at producing the so-called 'scissor' mouth, where the six upper incisors project only slightly beyond the incisors of the lower jaw, sitting closely over them and producing a perfect bite. This type of bite is superior to others, as in combat a dog tends to strike downwards and sideways. If a Stafford is badly undershot he is severely handicapped, and his bite becomes more bruising than cutting.

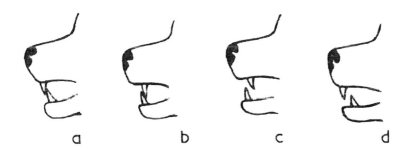

(a) Ideal Stafford mouth showing correct 'scissor' bite, with the six upper incisor teeth fitting closely over the lower incisors
(b) A slightly undershot jaw, with one or more of the lower incisors fitting closely over the upper incisors
(c) A badly undershot jaw. The lower jaw protrudes so much that the lower incisors do not touch the upper incisors
(d) A badly overshot jaw, the upper jaw protruding; often associated with a long weak muzzle

Do not be misled if you are told that a particular undershot stud dog of yesteryear produced a number of top-class specimens, all with 'perfect mouths' (less is heard of the number of undershot progeny produced). This fact is not at variance with the laws of genetics; the fault he carried may possibly reappear in future generations. In the early days of my association with the breed most enthusiasts seemed responsible enough to discard all undershot specimens from their breeding programmes, and undershot jaws began to disappear. It may be because of the gratuitous advice of a few voluble experts that the situation appears to have reversed. It is interesting to note that the Working Party, appointed by the Kennel Club to study breed standards, considers that, as the dental formula of all breeds is the same, 'the ideal bite is the scissor bite and that *all* breeds would be better for aiming to get as near to the ideal as possible'. Our hope for the future is that newcomers to the breed will carefully consider the consequences of breeding from undershot stock.

There must be considerable pressures on owners of undershot bitches to breed from them. If you must, please attempt to trace the origin of the fault, choose a suitable stud dog which shows three generations of sound dentition – and hope! Under no circumstances use an undershot stud dog; there are plenty of good stud dogs available with sound mouths.

Neck

A muscular, rather short neck is necessary in both Standards, but the present Standard requires the neck to be 'clean in outline and gradually widen towards the shoulders'. This kind of neck is seen on our best Staffords and in my view contributes towards a 'classic' appearance. Obviously a powerful head is of limited value to a fighting dog if it is mounted on a weak neck. In addition, there is little doubt that the length, girth and shape of the neck all play a significant part in providing a pleasing silhouette. It is interesting to note that in the original Standard, the neck, one of only five sections of the anatomy mentioned, warranted 10 points out of a total of 100 in the scale of points.

Forequarters

The present Standard amplifies the original: not only should legs be straight, they should be set rather wide apart and there should be no looseness at the shoulders.

Evidence of weakness at the pasterns, a fault that unfortunately is not uncommon in some of our dogs, particularly those that are overweight, detracts from general appearance; weak pasterns are often associated with splay feet, which together contribute a real threat to agility.

The Standard also requires the feet to turn out a little but recently there have been suggestions that feet should be 'straight to the front' as from an aesthetic viewpoint this may be preferred. As long as the Standard remains in its present form, feet must turn out a little, but, like a great deal of wording in the

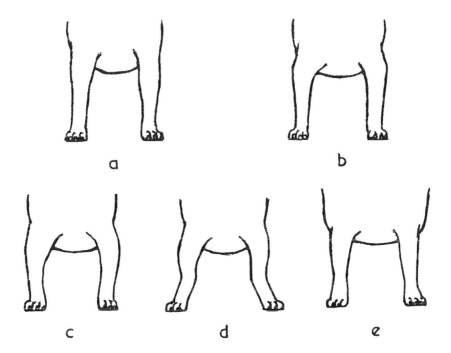

(a) Straight, well boned legs, the correct distance apart, showing no weakness at the pasterns. Feet turn out a little as required by the Standard
(b) Legs 'out at the elbows', clearly pointing outwards
(c) Loose shoulders, recognisable by a tendency to cross or 'plait' the feet when walking
(d) Exaggerated weak front, showing lighter bone and 'Chippendale' legs
(e) Overloaded shoulders

Standard, 'little' is liable to various interpretations. I know of no practical reason why a significant turn-out of feet is advantageous, though a slight amount of turn could perhaps help a fighting dog to propel itself forward; certainly a very slight amount provides a more pleasing front elevation than pronounced turn-out.

Body
A short, straight back is preferable, for the obvious reason that it is usually a strong back. Longer backs, erroneously thought less undesirable in brood bitches, are sometimes weak backs, often associated with long heads and long tails, none of which are to be recommended.

Level toplines are emphasised in the current Standard and usually denote correct spinal anatomy. As dogs become older

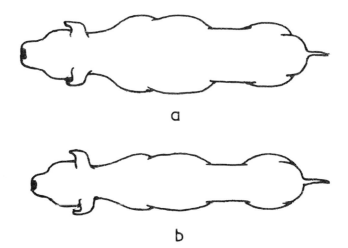

(a) Good development, with broad shoulders, well sprung ribs and rather light loins

(b) Undesirably thin ribs and shoulders

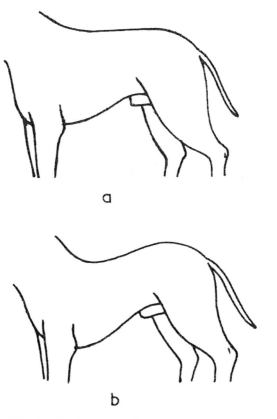

(a) Good back with level top line

(b) Roach back with pronounced dip behind the shoulders

they sometimes develop a 'saddle-back', a condition which, together with the 'roach-back', is undesirable. The rib cage, which provides protection for the heart and lungs, should be large enough for their full development, and there should be a deep brisket, well-developed chest and large shoulders. The general body appearance should be of tremendous strength commensurate with its size, without any trace of excess fat. In the original Standard, the scale of points allocated 25 points out of 100 for the body.

Hindquarters

It is essential that the hindquarters of a Staffordshire Bull Terrier should be well muscled and let down at the hocks, and that the stifles should be well bent. A fighting dog needs to be able to launch himself from a well-balanced base, and the Standard obviously took account of this.

The Standard also specifies that 'legs should be parallel when viewed from behind', and this places at a disadvantage those dogs that are 'cow-hocked' or 'in-toed'. Either of these two conditions restricts free rear movement, and there is therefore a sound practical reason why they should be faulted. After the breed achieved Kennel Club recognition in 1935, there was an improvement in the rear movement, and straight stifles became

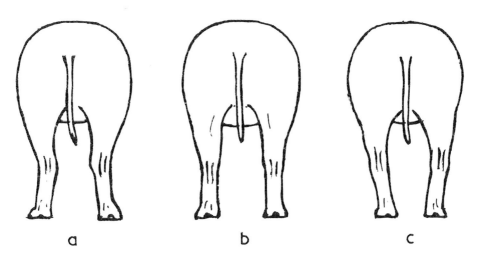

(a) 'Cow-hocked' hindquarters; (b) ideal rear view; (c) 'in-toed' hindquarters less prevalent; however they seem to have re-appeared, and breeders owning bitches with this fault should be especially careful in selecting a stud dog so that the fault will eventually be completely eliminated. A slipped patella is often the result of straight stifles, and this condition causes lameness, especially in adverse weather conditions, and usually develops into a chronic fault which is difficult and often impossible to cure.

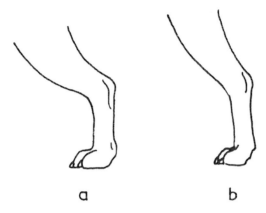

a   b

(a) Well bent stifle providing good power base; (b) straight stifle

It is almost impossible for judges accurately to assess rear movement solely from behind, and consequently some exhibits that are not completely sound in this respect occasionally do better than they should in the show-ring. Aspiring judges should always view the movement of exhibits from the side as well as from the front and rear, as this is the only way to establish the dog's complete movement.

Feet
Although not immediately apparent, there is, as with most facets of the Standard, a pragmatic reason why feet should be well-padded, strong and of medium size. Dogs possessing thin flat feet or splayed toes are at a considerable disadvantage in a sporting context; over-large feet tend to be associated with cumbersome movement. They are a fault which seems to be appearing more often in the breed at present, and is generally congenital. Breeders should attempt to eliminate it. The requirement that

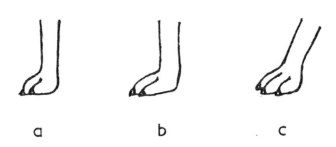

a   b   c

(a) Well knuckled, compact foot; (b) foot too flat and thin; (c) weak pasterns

feet should turn out a little has been considered above. Splayed forefeet, often associated with weak pasterns, are possibly one of the worst faults in this context and together present a less attractive appearance as well as a physical handicap.

The importance of feet and legs to agility is reflected in the scale of points accompanying the original Standard; 15 points were to be given to them.

Tail

Although it has been stated that the tail was a useful rear steering mechanism in a fighting dog, enabling him to turn more effectively, I find it difficult to subscribe to this view. There is a great variation in the sizes and shapes of tails in the Staffordshire Bull Terrier and little doubt that the traditional oldfashioned pump-handle tail of medium size, carried low, improves the appearance of any dog. 'Gay' tails certainly detract from general appearance, and short, badly curled tails are clearly aesthetically objectionable. Equally, the over-long tail is less pleasing and, as stated earlier, is often associated with a long muzzle and a long back.

The allocation of only 5 points in the original Standard's scale of points indicates the importance of the tail from a practical viewpoint.

Coat

In common with most animals, Staffords will grow a longer, coarser coat if subject to extremely cold conditions; this is simply nature's way of providing adequate covering. Ideally a dog should be kept indoors if a very short, smooth coat is required, but this is not always desirable or possible. Nevertheless long, coarse coats are to be discouraged, and a smooth, short coat, close to the skin, exhibiting the bloom of a healthy dog, certainly improves its general appearance.

Colour

The present Standard added blue to the original colours of red, fawn, white and black, or any shade of brindle. Some controversy surrounds blue Staffords, and even today this colour is by no means common. Suggestions have been made that the introduction of the colour was through Blue Pauls, a breed of dog supposed to have been introduced into the British Isles by the pirate Paul Jones. It appears that Blue Pauls, which were most common in an area of Scotland to the north of Glasgow, were certainly used as fighting dogs by Scottish gypsies, among others. The more popular theory is that most so-called blue Staffordshire Bull Terriers are really blue brindles, in which the striping is so faint that the coat appears to be blue. It has been suggested that the colour blue is a diluted black, the pigment granules being much less numerous than they are in dense hair; thus a dog in which the pigment granules are weakly concentrated would appear to be blue. As dogs with dilute coat colours are often associated with light eyes, they are in general less popular with exhibitors. Paradoxically the all-white Stafford, which is far from popular, often has a dark eye.

Although only black-and-tan and liver are colours not to be encouraged, there is little doubt that most enthusiasts have a colour preference. White markings on any dog, whether it is red or brindle, on certain areas of the anatomy enhance its general appearance. Although this may be a subjective judgement, many people looking at a show-ring full of dogs will have their gaze immediately attracted to those with pied coats. The judge may find that any of these animals possess faults which will debar them from competing for the major awards; my point is that one's eyes are often directed to this colour or to those dogs which have their main coat colour relieved by white.

Perhaps there is an analogy which is well known in the world of advertising: gold on a black background or black on a gold background is one of the most eye-catching colour combinations.

However, if you have the opportunity of owning any really good specimen of the breed, don't be put off by the colour – unless it is black-and-tan or liver!

Weight and size
The original Standard was more flexible than the current Standard, as it simply asked for a dog 'standing about 15 to 18in high at the shoulder', and a weight of 'dogs 28lb to 38lb, bitches 4lb less'. There was no stipulation relating the weights to the heights, but this requirement is explicit in the present Standard. It is now stated categorically that dogs should weigh between 12·7 and 17·24k (28–38lb) and bitches between 10·89 and 15·42k (24–34lb), with the height (at the shoulder) being 35·56–40·64cm (14–16in), *these heights being related to weights*. (The italics are mine.) If, therefore, a Stafford is to comply exactly to the weight and size clause at present stipulated it should be in accord with the following table.

Dogs		Bitches	
Height	*Weight*	*Height*	*Weight*
35·56cm (14in)	12·70k (28lb)	35·56cm (14in)	10·89k (24lb)
36·83cm (14½in)	13·89k (30½lb)	36·83cm (14½in)	12·07k (26½lb)
38·10cm (15in)	14·97k (33lb)	38·10cm (15in)	13·15k (29lb)
39·37cm (15½in)	16·15k (35½lb)	39·37cm (15½in)	14·34k (31½lb)
40·64cm (16in)	17·24k (38lb)	40·64cm (16in)	15·42k (34lb)

Most observers of the breed would I think agree that this part of the Standard has become a nonsense. Winning specimens at today's championship shows are much heavier than the weight laid down in the Standard, and a well-balanced dog standing 40·64cm (16in) at the shoulder can often weigh well over 18·12k (40lb). Some alteration should be made to this clause as most judges have ignored it for so long that it has ceased to have any real meaning. It would be preferable to indicate a desired height with no weight limit but with the proviso that there should be an impression of great substance commensurate with size. I would add that dogs should look masculine and bitches feminine, but this and other suggested alterations to the Standard are matters that must be considered at length and in depth first. At present there is so much opposition to any proposed amendment that it seems that the current Standard will continue for the foreseeable future.

Faults

The 1935 Standard detailed specific faults that were to be penalised – Dudley nose, light or pink eyes (rims), tail too long or badly curled, badly undershot or overshot mouths – but none that debarred any dog from winning any prize.

The present Standard, however, differentiates between faults that are to be 'penalised in accordance with their severity' and those that debar an exhibit from winning any prize. Those faults to be penalised in accordance with their severity include the light or pink eyes and tail malformation mentioned in the original Standard as well as non-conformation with weight and height limits, undershot or overshot mouths and full-drop or prick ears. The major faults debarring a dog from winning any prize whatsoever are a Dudley (pink) nose, and a badly undershot or overshot mouth. The badly undershot mouth, which was quite common in early specimens of the breed, is defined as 'where the lower jaw protrudes to such an extent that the incisors of the lower jaw do not touch those of the upper jaw'. A great deal of controversy surrounds undershot mouths and certainly some judges appear to be more lenient than others when assessing this fault.

Kennel Club Standards now contain the additional stipulation that all male animals should have two apparently normal testicles fully descended into the scrotum. Both the monorchid, or more correctly the unilateral cryptorchid, that is a dog with only one testicle descended into the scrotum, and the cryptorchid, in which neither testicle has descended, have conditions which can be transmitted. The cryptorchid is usually sterile but under no circumstances should a monorchid, which can reproduce, or cryptorchid be used for breeding purposes.

Perhaps a chapter entitled 'Development of the Breed' would be incomplete without reference to the late H. N. Beilby, whose work on a system of lines and families of the breed is referred to even today. His book *The Staffordshire Bull Terrier*, first published in 1943, is now a collector's item and the most readable and authentic book so far on the breed. With the tremendous growth in popularity of the Staffordshire Bull Terrier over the past thirty-five years, however, it would require a specialist volume and tremendous research to continue his comprehensive system of lines and families, although individual breeders no doubt can trace back the pedigree of their progeny using his original system.

Since 1948 there has been a steady development of existing breed clubs and a growth of new ones. There are now fifteen Staffordshire Bull Terrier Breed Clubs operating throughout the British Isles. A complete list of these together with the names, addresses and telephone numbers of the secretaries is given in Appendix 2. Most breed clubs have as their objects the desire to foster an interest in the breed, to enable enthusiasts to exchange news and views and to hold shows and other events. By 1950 the five Breed Clubs then existing in England had formed a Joint Advisory Council, the forerunner of the present breed co-ordinating body, which has the rather grandiose title of 'The Staffordshire Bull Terrier Breed Council of Great Britain and Northern Ireland'. Further information on the Breed Council is given in Chapter 10, 'The Contemporary Scene'.

4

STOCK SELECTION

The selection of a dog, at whatever age, is a serious business and should be approached with caution even by the well-established enthusiast; it is even more difficult for the beginner. Obviously the experienced breeder and exhibitor is at an advantage when selecting stock – although most would probably admit to occasional errors of judgement – but the beginner has often to be guided by the vendor or the breeder when making his choice. Indeed, if the beginner is intent on purchasing a puppy, which seems the most popular method of entering the breed, he should endeavour to enlist experienced assistance before buying. Purchasing a puppy at eight weeks old, and this is the absolute minimum age that one should be bought, is something of a lottery. However, by applying his knowledge and experience to the transaction, the experienced breeder can reduce the odds substantially. It is essential to know personally, or at least have some knowledge of, the sire and dam of the litter from which the selection is to be made; ideally one should also know a great deal about the grand-sires and grand-dams. Although this knowledge would probably be of small value to the beginner, it would be of inestimable value to the expert.

At this point let me sound a note of warning about pedigrees. The word is derived from the French *pied de grue*, meaning 'crane's foot', which symbolises the resemblance of a written pedigree to the long spreading feet of this large wading bird. On a printed pedigree form may appear three, four or even five generations of the antecedents of a particular dog; in itself the form is valueless apart from its commercial value in selling the dog to an uninformed public!

The pedigree is of real use only if it conveys meaningful information; this presupposes that the person inspecting the document is aware of the virtues and faults of the dogs named on it. It is fully useful only if it conveys knowledge, either personal or recorded, of *all* the dogs mentioned therein. In practice this is often impossible, and the best that can be achieved is personal knowledge of *most* of the dogs mentioned. Such information would include the sizes of the dogs, their colours, their main virtues and faults, together with any specific points about them which are not easily learned even by physical examination, including temperamental factors and other propensities. The pedigree form reflects the relationship of the dogs and the degree of inbreeding, line breeding or outcrossing that has taken place.

If a long-established breeder is sufficiently capable of, and dedicated to, producing a number of generations of his own stock, he is at a decided advantage; indeed he has a unique opportunity of forecasting with a fair degree of accuracy how his puppies are likely to look at full maturity. (This subject will be dealt with later when considering the problems of breeding.)

Some enthusiasts when selecting puppies have a tendency to look at specific points of the anatomy rather than the puppy as a whole. One may concentrate on a large skull or a dome-shaped skull, another on a short muzzle, yet another on a short back. All may be important, but every facet of the dog should be examined in detail before finalising the purchase.

There is one unusual method of attempting to evaluate puppies; it seems to work for some, but geneticists do not approve, and scientifically they are right. The theory is that it is preferable to assess the puppies within two or three days of their birth rather than attempt to analyse them during their growing period. The proponents of this method say it is possible to see the dogs in a 'silhouette' form from which they can assess the likely final outline on maturity. Individual factors can be examined later at leisure. At this early stage, notes are made of the possible faults and virtues of each puppy, but no further assessment is attempted during the first few months of their lives when they can change drastically. It is claimed that the first assessment is usually more correct than any intermediate assessments, although this is not to suggest of course that they are always right! There is always some risk in attempting to assess a dog before maturity; it must however be done, and experience helps.

Mouths and hindquarters should be especially carefully examined. I have dealt elsewhere with these topics, but it should be re-emphasised that badly undershot mouths and straight stifles, two important defects in a fighting dog, are still seen in the breed, to what I consider to be an unacceptable level. Caution is advised if there is any tendency at all towards an undershot mouth; it will almost certainly get worse rather than better. Straight stifles can sometimes be identified in a young puppy, but it is easier to do so when the puppies are playing together; this fault then becomes more apparent. Faulty rear movement generally denotes anatomical faults in a Stafford, and a fighting dog with weak hindquarters is placed at a decided disadvantage, as he has no sound base from which to propel himself.

If the puppy is male, its genitals should be examined, as the Standard now stipulates that all males should have two apparently normal testicles fully descended into the scrotum. If in doubt consult an experienced breeder or a veterinary surgeon.

Different breeds of dog mature at different ages; even within individual breeds there may be differing times of maturity. It is not unusual for Staffordshire Bull Terriers to be three or more years old before they attain full maturity. In my experience, Staffords do not appear to reach their mental peak until some time after achieving physical maturity: I must confess, however, that this view is not based on any scientific research.

The combination of these factors adds to the problems of puppy selection, but generally one must look for 'structural' faults, which will remain with the puppy during its life and be perpetuated in a breeding programme; normally such stock would not be acceptable to the purchaser. However, it is not much comfort if one purchases a comparatively sound puppy completely lacking in breed type. Normally I look for shortness of muzzle, back and tail, and make a detailed examination of mouths and hindquarters, but equally I insist on seeing not only the dam but the sire. Ideally one should inspect the grandparents too, but this is not always possible.

When selecting a puppy at about eight weeks, the usual age for transfer of ownership, I would concentrate on the following:

Body Short, with deep brisket and short straight tail.
Legs Showing good bone. Straight front legs with well bent stifles at the rear.
Head Short muzzle, a defined stop and a good girth of skull. Well placed round eye.
Mouth The top incisors fitting snugly over the lower incisors and showing this level along all the incisors. If the milk teeth are correctly aligned it is probable, although not certain, that permanent dentition will be acceptable. Be suspicious if the lower jaw shows any indication of protruding beyond the upper.
Temperament It is virtually impossible to assess temperament from visual examination. Look for a friendly, active and lively puppy at this stage.

Of course a great deal of the risk can be eliminated by selecting an adult dog rather than a puppy. It must be remembered however, that the Stafford is a slow-maturing breed and specimens that may seem little better than reasonable show prospects at nine months of age can turn out to be potential champions a year later. Breeders usually dispose of their litters at between eight and ten weeks, retaining only those puppies they wish to keep for exhibition or for their future breeding programmes. It follows, therefore, that adult stock offered for sale may include those that have not quite reached their owners' aspirations. Occasionally an owner may give up his interest in the breed and dispose of all of his stock, or there may be other legitimate reasons why a particularly good specimen is available for sale; unfortunately such opportunities rarely occur.

Many beginners do not know whether to choose a dog or a bitch puppy. The consensus of opinion seems to favour a bitch, especially if you contemplate breeding. If a dog puppy turns out to have major faults, which make a successful show career improbable, it will not be in great demand as a stud dog. If, however, a relatively sound bitch eventually proves unsuitable for exhibition, it can be used for breeding purposes; careful selection of a stud dog may produce typical puppies which could be of show standard. Eventually, by careful selection, an acceptable strain may evolve and many successful breeders have commenced their operations in this way.

One perennial problem facing the owners of bitches of any

breed is that of the oestrum, or heat, which may cause anxiety for three weeks or so twice a year. It has been said however that owners of romantic stud dogs face this problem each day of the year! It is very much an individual choice; I would be happy with a good specimen of either sex, but for most people a bitch is preferable.

Finally, having selected your puppy, or indeed your adult dog, immediate steps should be taken to have it registered at the Kennel Club, if this has not already been done; if it has, then the records should be amended to show the new owner's name. It is the usual practice for breeders, especially those with an affix (a name only that breeder can use), to register all puppies before sale. In this event a Kennel Club Form 6, 'Transfer of a Registered Dog', should be obtained, either from the breeder or from the Kennel Club, completed, signed by both old and new owners and forwarded to the Kennel Club at 1 Clarges Street, Piccadilly, London W1Y 8AB, with the current fee. If the dog has not been registered previously, Form 1, or Form 1A in certain cases, should be used, and signed by both breeder and owner of the sire of the litter.

There is occasionally some delay in applications being confirmed by the Kennel Club. If exhibitors wish to show their dogs before documentation is returned they can still do so by marking the initials N.A.F. (name applied for) or T.A.F. (transfer applied for) after the name of their dog on their entry forms.

The popularity of the Stafford has resulted in its export from Britain to many other countries, and breeders willing to sell their dogs to owners overseas will need to know the formalities required when exporting a dog. Different countries have their own regulations concerning the import of livestock, and breeders can obtain more detailed information from the Ministry of Agriculture, Fisheries & Food (Animal Health Division), Government Buildings, Hook Rise South, Tolworth, Surbiton, Surrey (telephone: 01-337 6611).

Export pedigrees are available from the Kennel Club at a nominal charge, which varies according to the country to which the dog is going. To qualify for an export pedigree a dog must have three generations of registered breeding and itself be registered. The registration must be transferred to the new owner, giving his overseas address, but the transfer form can be signed by the vendor on behalf of the purchaser. Many of the exported Staffords go to the United States of America, where the person receiving the dog must be an American citizen if it is to enter the United States duty-free; in this case too the pedigree must accompany the dog.

Applications made to the Kennel Club for an export pedigree should be accompanied by a signed certificate regarding cryptorchidism and a completed transfer form, together with the appropriate fee. Exporters have found the Kennel Club most helpful, and the staff are able to issue export pedigrees within a relatively short time. Obviously it is best for everyone concerned if applications can be submitted well in advance of the export date.

Although most of the information required regarding export can be obtained either from the Ministry of Agriculture, Fisheries & Food or from the Kennel Club, a list of the controlling bodies responsible for exhibition dogs in overseas countries where Staffords are kept is given in Appendix 3. Overseas buyers wishing to buy a Stafford from England would be well advised to purchase their stock from a 'legitimate' breeder; he or she is likely to be well known within the area where his breeding establishment is situated, so it is a double insurance to contact the secretary of one of the fifteen breed clubs concerned, who may be able to give helpful advice. When purchasing a Stafford from Britain, an overseas buyer has to pay not only for the dog but for the freight costs, insurance, export licences, export documents, veterinary fees, health certificates where necessary, Kennel Club transfer forms and a number of other incidental expenses.

There are firms in England that specialise in the export of dogs, and some breeders use their services. In any event, details of the complete transaction, preferably in writing, should be clearly understood by both vendor and purchaser before the dog is sent abroad. This involves forwarding a copy of the pedigree, together with a good photograph of the dog and a statement of the agreed price to the prospective buyer, plus the agreement regarding the payment of the various expenses mentioned in the previous paragraph.

Obviously many breeders are reluctant to sell their best stock, either at home or abroad, but recently some quite good Staffords have gone overseas, which is one of the ways in which Staffords can be improved round the world. Overseas breeders are of course producing some good stock themselves, and eventually some may feel that further importation from the United Kingdom is unnecessary. It seems likely, though, that there will always be some international movement of Staffordshire Bull Terriers, with UK breeders being the principal exporters in the foreseeable future.

5

MANAGEMENT AND FEEDING

Once you have acquired a Staffordshire Bull Terrier, you must decide whether it should be kept in the home or in kennels. Most Staffords are kept indoors where they can be better companions to their owners – and can act as a deterrent to possible intruders.

Puppies quickly follow a routine if the minimum of training is given, and it is not difficult to find some warm, dry place in the house which will make suitable sleeping quarters. Obviously they should be kept out of draughts, and, if necessary, a bench or something similar should be provided to raise them from floor level. Unless it interferes unduly with domestic arrangements, I prefer to keep dogs indoors where they can more easily integrate with the family.

If you keep a number of dogs and undertake breeding operations, kennelling is essential. There are no really large kennels of Staffordshire Bull Terriers, fortunately, and my hope is that there never will be. The average breeder may keep two or three bitches and perhaps a stud dog; a breeder who keeps more than six adult Staffordshire Bull Terriers is very much the exception. I say 'fortunately' because I firmly believe that the Staffordshire Bull Terrier is a breed that requires to spend some time indoors with human company. When we were breeding from our dogs and they were all kennelled, each of them spent part of the day indoors and visibly looked forward to the occasion. If the choice has to be kennels, they should be as large as possible and at least 2m (6ft 6in) high so that the owner can go in easily and move about comfortably within the dogs' quarters. Ideally there should be both concrete and grass runs available, surrounded by an unclimbable fence of a minimum height of 2m (6ft 6in); often this is not possible, and most owners and breeders seem to manage well with various degrees of improvisation.

Anyone owning a dog for the first time may be confused by the methods of feeding used, and there are certainly some feeding faddists in the canine world. My own view is that feeding should be as simple as possible. Specialist producers of dog foods now supply a wide variety of products containing all the essentials for a dog's wellbeing. Generally such proprietary foods are easily prepared and need only be fed to adult dogs once a day; puppies require special treatment. I have used a number of these preparations, all of which contained the necessary protein, carbohydrate, vitamins and minerals essential to a dog's health, and all have proved successful. Obviously some are better than others, and often it is a matter of experience and personal choice. The only reservation I have about using one variety permanently is that dogs, like humans, occasionally appreciate a change of diet, and, with some thought, this can be easily arranged. We use a dry 'complete' dog food, consisting of animal protein and cereals together with essential vitamins and minerals. Boiling water or meat stock is poured over the food and mixed to a crumbly consistency; finally we add approximately 8oz of canned meat. Permutations in the canned meat (beef, mutton, offal) ensure some variety in the diet.

If a puppy is acquired at eight weeks of age it should be fed four or five times each day until it is about four months old. Regular meal times are desirable but can usually be arranged to fit into the owner's other commitments. We found it convenient to feed our puppies at the times of our own meals. Typical meals could be as follows:

8.00a.m. breakfast Basically a milk-based meal. There are numerous proprietary brands of powdered milk especially manufactured for dogs, but there are cheaper methods of feeding. We have an arrangement with a local pharmacist who sells us 'time-expired' baby foods at a fraction of the retail price. Although based on cow's milk, they have additives that make them more nutritious. They may be served alone at first and suitable cereals added as the puppy progresses.

12.00 noon lunch This should be a meat-based meal. Lean meat can be bought, chopped into small pieces and puppy biscuit

Cockney Charlie Lloyd and Champion Pilot. They earned a sizeable income in the USA after emigrating around 1868

Tridwr Dicey Riley at five months. Owned and bred by Tom Fletcher in 1979, out of Ch Cottfol Princess of Tridwr by Ch Pitbul Red Regent

Ch Benext Beau, owned and bred by Mr and Mrs Ken Bailey. This dog gained 18 challenge certificates – a breed record

meal, of which there is a wide choice available, added. Gravy or some other meat stock can then be poured over the whole meal. Alternatively, one of the 'complete dog foods' which are now available can be used. Some of these, scientifically blended to include every dietary requirement, seem to produce excellent results and are often more economical.

4.00p.m. tea   Another milk-based meal similar to breakfast. As a change an occasional egg can be offered.

8.00p.m. dinner   The meat-based lunch meal should be repeated. If fresh or tinned meat is being fed this can be varied with fish, taking special care to extract all bones.

As the puppy's stomach is relatively small at this stage it should not be distended unduly, and meals should, therefore, be small and frequent.

If one of the complete dog foods is being used, it should already contain adequate amounts of vitamins and minerals; if not, certain additives may be necessary. First-time owners occasionally become obsessed with additives and waste a great deal of money buying a wide range of extra vitamins and minerals that are already present in their dog's diet. My own view is that normally the addition of reasonable amounts of calcium and cod-liver oil to the diet are all that is necessary. Cod-liver oil and halibut oil are good cheap sources of vitamins A and D. Vitamin A is necessary for growth, and vitamin D must be present, if only in small quantities, for the full utilisation of calcium, essential for the proper formation of bones and teeth.

For owners who prefer to be more individualistic in their feeding, it should be emphasised that all dogs need adequate amounts of protein, carbohydrates, vitamins and minerals. Many diets that are not scientifically based succeed in meeting these requirements; if, however, a puppy's progress does not proceed normally, then it may be due to a dietary deficiency and the situation should be immediately investigated.

Proteins of animal origin are found in all types of meat, offal, cheese, fish and eggs. Many of these foods contain adequate amounts of vitamins A, B, D and F, and also minerals. However, fresh meat is expensive, although economies can be made by purchasing in bulk from specialist wholesalers and freezing until required. Care should be taken in feeding certain types of offal as a permanent substitute to meat without the addition of supplements.

Carbohydrates are usually fed in biscuit form and contribute towards energy and warmth. For the owner with only one dog, surplus wholemeal bread, dried out in the oven to form rusks, is quite suitable. Over-feeding of carbohydrates, especially in later life when the dog is less active, is to be avoided as it can lead to obesity.

The vitamins required by a dog will usually be found in the normal diet, but, during puppyhood especially, supplements should be fed to ensure that there is no vitamin deficiency. Vitamins A and D have already been mentioned, and vitamin B in the form of brewer's yeast could also be introduced. Vetzyme, a well-known proprietary brand of tablet containing the vitamin B complex, is popular among dog owners and usually appreciated by the dogs.

Minerals such as calcium, phosphorus and iron are usually present in the diets previously described; some owners introduce a mineral supplement and a popular proprietary brand is Stress, which is marketed by Phillips Yeast Products.

By the time the puppy has reached the age of about four months its meals can be reduced to three a day. At this age the growth rate is reaching its peak and permanent teething is beginning, and the puppy needs a larger intake of the appropriate foods; my own name for this period is the 'calcium and cod-liver oil stage'. This permanent-teething stage is regarded by some as the most critical in the life of a dog, a period when, in the past, distemper and other infections tended to attack. Modern veterinary science has lessened the seriousness of infections, but nevertheless good management is still essential.

As the quality and placement of teeth are such important aspects of a sporting dog, and especially of a breed developed for organised fighting, the Stafford's dentition should be described. It has forty-two permanent teeth, twenty in the upper jaw and twenty-two in the lower jaw. In each lateral half of the upper jaw there are three incisors, one canine, four premolars and two molars; in the lower jaw the arrangement is the same except that there is an extra molar in each lateral half.

I have already mentioned the incisor teeth; in the Stafford the six top incisors should fit closely over the six lower incisors in what is generally known as a scissor mouth. Incisor teeth are basically the cutting teeth, used to divide food, and behind them are the well-developed canine teeth, large, conical in shape and used for piercing and tearing. Finally, to the rear of the canines, are premolars followed by the larger molars, which together are used for grinding.

At about seven months of age meals can be reduced to two each day, a light meal either in the morning or at noon and the main meat-based meal in the evening. There is no need slavishly to follow some textbook advice on feeding an adult dog. The times of feeding are not as important as the regularity of meals, and many experienced dog owners feed only one meal a day, usually in the evening. I have used a proprietary 'complete dog food' for some time and find that my dogs thrive on it, but there are equally good alternatives. Do, however, change the diet occasionally; and, unlike some owners, I believe a constant supply of fresh water should be available.

Some form of exercise is necessary for all dogs; it is essential if a healthy, typical Staffordshire Bull Terrier is to be reared. Unexercised dogs, especially those that are over-fed, soon become flabby and more susceptible to a wide variety of ailments. Unfortunately many adult Staffords seem to be inherently lazy and, if not motivated, will be content to lie for hours in front of a warm fire or in some other comfortable spot, especially as they get older. If only one dog is kept the problem is often more acute, and a positive attempt must be made to ensure that the dog has adequate exercise. The daily walk, exploring new territory on every possible occasion, is enjoyable and beneficial, but the old-fashioned game of throwing and retrieving a ball is popular with most Staffords. We have an eleven-year-old bitch who even now can retrieve small tree trunks weighing nearly as much as she does; she seems to retrieve the thing more easily than I can manage to throw it! A word of warning, however, when throwing a stick for a Stafford; dogs often become so involved in a game, that, in their enthusiasm, they may occasionally include your finger as well as the stick in their jaws unless adequate care is taken. It is also unwise to play such games with more than one dog at the same time even though each may have its own stick, as injuries can result from excited dogs turning quickly when holding such a 'weapon'.

Although readers may find it difficult to equate games with obedience training, certain Staffords we have owned appear to enjoy this discipline in its basic form. At least one of our dogs, which we did not attempt to train until it was nearly four years old, became quite proficient in some of the basic 'sequences'. Certainly it seemed to enjoy the training, but whether this was due to the extra attention it received in the process I am not sure. There are of course a number of Staffords which have been trained to quite a high degree of efficiency and some have attained awards at working trials and obedience classes conducted under Kennel Club regulations.

It is beyond the scope of this book to deal with obedience training, but some basic training is essential for every puppy and its owner. House training certainly comes into this category, and fortunately most Staffords are easily trained in this respect. It must be remembered, however, that an eight-weeks-old puppy needs to be put outside after each meal; in bad weather a box filled with sawdust or other suitable litter can be used. Endeavour to avoid any accidents, as puppies incline to give repeat performances in the same place if the smell of urine is present. The scent must be eliminated as soon as possible by disinfecting or other means. The current thinking is that rewards are more effective than punishments in puppy training, but I have found that gentle punishment delivered lightly with a roll of newspaper is also effective.

If only one dog is to be kept there will be times when it will be left alone. At first it may whine or howl, and many owners will be tempted to return to pacify their pet; this is a mistake. Only return when the puppy has stopped whining, and then reward it with praise or maybe a delicacy. Owners must ensure that they and not their dogs win these early 'trials of strength'.

One aspect of training which seems difficult for some Stafford owners is that of walking their charges on a lead. Staffords are usually very strong, active dogs, eager to explore new territory as quickly as possible. Using a choke collar with 'trial and error' methods is often laborious and exhausting. The alternative is to introduce a thin collar to the puppy when it is about three months of age. After it has accepted the collar, attach a long piece of strong cord and allow the puppy to walk – or probably run – some distance before it feels the restraint. When its progress has been halted, call the puppy to you, rewarding it with praise if it returns of its own accord. If the puppy refuses, gently pull the cord; if this method fails it is necessary to go to the puppy and repeat the exercise. Eventually it will learn to return, and this is the signal to substitute a lead.

Puppies should be trained individually, and any form of pulling on the lead firmly dealt with, if necessary by the use of a rolled newspaper. A sharp pull on the lead, together with a suitable word of command such as 'stay' or 'back', may be adequate for some breeds, but the Stafford often needs the added deterrent of the rolled newspaper. Again, adequate praise should be given each time some degree of success is achieved. Lead training is essential if you propose to show your Stafford, but this should be supplemented by attending the training classes that are held by specialist breed clubs and by many general canine societies. A list of breed clubs is given in Appendix 2, and the addresses of secretaries of general societies can be obtained from the Kennel Club, 1 Clarges Street, Piccadilly, London W1Y 8AB.

May I conclude these sections on feeding and exercise by mentioning bones – delicacies for dogs to eat and play with! Most Staffords love a bone; besides being an object to gnaw and eat, it becomes a treasure to be hidden and guarded and a plaything to excite the imagination. Unfortunately a dog's teeth can be displaced by injudicious use of bones. There appears to be a wide range of opinions among breeders and exhibitors on this subject; some will not allow bones at all, others feel that bones should not be given until a dog is fully matured, while others take the view that, apart from poultry and similar bones, all are acceptable.

Some suggest that the best bones are the large knuckle bones, which cannot be crushed; others firmly believe that this type may cause teeth displacement and only give the softer, rib-type bone.

No general rule can be applied, but certainly I have seen teeth displaced in puppyhood and even in later life, by dogs regularly chewing on apparently impenetrable knuckle-joint bones. Of course, if a dog's jaw is properly undershot its lower incisors will in any event protrude to some extent in front of the top incisor teeth; it is true, however, that a dog with correct jaw formation can acquire misplaced incisors as a result of being given bones.

Any chapter on management would be incomplete without reference to the health of the Stafford. Fortunately the breed does not suffer to any great extent from genetic diseases such as hip dysplasia, which seems to affect the larger breeds. In lay terms this condition may be described as a degeneration of the hip socket which results in permanent lameness. As it is a complex hereditary condition it must be avoided at all costs.

The Stafford owner will almost certainly be concerned with roundworms. When a puppy is purchased at eight weeks of age it should already have been wormed three times — at three weeks, five weeks and seven weeks — and should, therefore, be worm-free when it is collected by its new owner. Any suspicion of worm infestation should be immediately investigated, however, and there are numerous efficient worm remedies available, which can be administered easily by the beginner. Many owners think it advisable to worm all dogs annually, not only for the dog's welfare but because of public concern regarding the possible effects of *Toxacara canis* (the veterinary term for the common roundworm) on humans. Cases occasionally occur of children incurring serious eye damage as a result of swallowing eggs from an infected dog's faeces left on grass where they play. Recently public attention has been focused on Burnley, where the local council decided to ban all dogs from public parks because of the dangers of this disease. Immediately dog owners in the town closed ranks, and a few purposely ignored the bylaw. The court's ruling was not in their favour, and they were faced with substantial costs, though dog owners throughout the country, through their clubs and societies, donated generously to the efforts of the dog press to raise funds to meet these costs. Parliament has not so far sanctioned further bylaws enabling any other local authority to invoke a similar ban.

Virus and bacterial infections are possibly the greatest threats to a dog's health. Owners of puppies are strongly recommended to have their dogs inoculated against the three serious infections of distemper (including para-distemper), canine virus hepatitis and leptrospiral jaundice; the inoculation can now be administered in one dose followed later by a booster injection.

A more serious disease which appeared in Britain only in 1979 is parvo-virus, which has since been exercising the minds of our veterinary researchers. Dogs have been immunised against this particular virus with feline dead enteritis vaccine and experiments are being carried out with feline live enteritis vaccine. Meanwhile the incidence of death, especially among younger stock, is alarming, and all dog owners hope that a universally effective vaccine can soon be found.

Staffords seem susceptible to a skin disease that usually appears on the neck or shoulders in the form of a dry circular patch about the size of a 5p piece. The hair falls out, and the dog is left with a bald area on its coat. Various theories, including that of a vitamin deficiency, have been advanced for the cause of this condition, and a wide variety of remedies attempted. The symptoms can be alarming as they resemble follicular mange; in my experience the condition is not serious and usually corrects itself within two or three months with the minimum of treatment.

Finally, although some experienced dog breeders are able to undertake a certain amount of medicinal work with their stock, beginners should be very cautious in this respect. The normal temperature of a dog is 38.5°C (101.4°F), taken in the anus with a suitable thermometer held in position for at least one minute. If the temperature rises to 39.4°C (103°F) or above, or if there is any doubt about a dog's health, then the services of a veterinary surgeon are necessary. It is certainly advisable to make the acquaintance of a vet as soon as possible if you own a dog; you can never anticipate when you may need him.

6
BREEDING

Having acquired a Stafford and seen it grow to adulthood, many bitch owners will feel disposed to commence breeding operations. Like most aspects of life, experience is of the essence, and newcomers should endeavour to enlist the aid of another enthusiast who is well versed in breeding Staffords. This should not be difficult if the newcomer becomes a member of his nearest specialist breed club.

Before choosing a stud dog, a detailed study of the pedigrees of the bitch and the potential sire should be made. Pedigrees are of real value only if information about all the dogs shown therein is available. Today many breeders attempt some form of line breeding, which, in over-simplified terms, means mating the bitch to a stud dog of the same line of dogs that produced her. The current choice of a stud dog is, unfortunately, not as simple as this, and line breeding, which is in any event a fairly generic term, is not the panacea for all breeding problems, although it is important.

An objective assessment of the bitch should first be made, and, if necessary, expert opinion invited to supplement the views of the owner. The virtues of the bitch should be recorded, but, perhaps more importantly, her faults should be carefully listed. She may, for example, be too tall and there may be a temptation to mate her to a smaller than average dog in order to correct this fault. This would be a grave error, as it would be compounding the original fault by introducing not one but two faults, that of too much height and that of too little height. If the bitch is too tall, a stud dog of the ideal height should be selected whose parents, and ideally grandparents too, were all of the correct height. This ideal may not be obtainable but it certainly should be the aim.

An analysis of the bitch's pedigree may indicate from which

antecedents her faults have derived; these faults should be noted and care taken to avoid repeating past errors by a positive attempt to eliminate the immediate progeny of such stock from breeding programmes. Eventually, by careful selection, a strain may be established that is free from major faults and dogs produced that are of similar appearance. This is the ultimate aim: the production of puppies that are themselves similar and that are as near the requirements of the Standard as possible.

The establishment of such a strain will certainly involve line breeding and at some juncture may include some degree of inbreeding. Inbreeding simply concentrates the characteristics already present and, if carried out intelligently, can often be of value. It must be remembered, however, that inbreeding not only concentrates the virtues, it also concentrates the faults. It is essential, therefore, that when inbreeding is contemplated, the stock should be good, typical, healthy dogs that are completely free from major faults. The most rigid selection of stock before embarking on any form of inbreeding cannot be over-emphasised.

Conversely a situation may be reached where an established strain produces progeny with certain recurring faults. It then becomes necessary to outcross, or to introduce new blood into the strain. Many consider that the crossing of two distinct strains is not likely to give good results immediately and that new blood should be introduced gradually. Although this may be generally true, certain circumstances may necessitate some form of outcross. Indeed, an initial outcross has often produced good puppies; it is when this stock is used for further breeding that problems may occur.

Finally, it should be remembered that a dog's success in the show-ring is no guarantee of its success as a sire; the advice previously given is equally applicable. As many as possible of the dog's antecendents should be investigated, and certainly information should be obtained about its sire and dam. It is possible, although not usual, for two very average parents to produce a really excellent dog; unfortunately the possibility of this dog passing on its virtues may not be so great!

Ideally the brood bitch should come from sound stock of good breed type and be correctly constructed herself. She should be healthy, well exercised and in hard condition; an over-fat bitch is more likely to have whelping troubles and is less likely to conceive.

Careful attention should be given to the choice of a stud dog and the temptation to use a particular dog because of its geographical proximity, or simply because one is friendly with the owner, should be resisted. The choice must depend on several factors, including the dog's success as a sire, his particular virtues and faults in relation to the bitch and a comparison of antecedents by reference to both pedigrees. Moreover, the stud dog should be in first-class condition, lean and hard. A stud dog should ideally be kept apart from any bitch in season until his services are required, as a bitch's scent can frustrate him to such an extent that he loses condition.

Having selected a stud dog well in advance, an arrangement must be made with the owner for a stud fee. Occasionally owners of stud dogs may accept a puppy from the litter in lieu of a fee; if the puppy is the pick of the litter such an arrangement may not be to the breeder's advantage. It must be understood that a stud fee is payable for the dog's services and does not depend on the arrival of a litter. In my experience, however, owners of Stafford stud dogs always offer a second free service if no pups arrive. Ideally a clear written agreement should be entered into; this may occasionally cause embarrassment, but it affords greater protection for the aggrieved party if a dispute occurs.

Occasionally, after making all arrangements well in advance, circumstances may arise that make a mating with the chosen stud dog impossible. Owners particularly desirous of breeding from their bitches at this time should have emergency plans available in the form of an alternative stud dog. Such planning may cause embarrassment, especially if the owner of a stud dog knows he is second choice, and it may be more prudent to have the stud dog of a friend as the 'reserve', but even then the dog should have much to commend it; if not, it is probably better to wait until the bitch comes into season again.

It is generally accepted that a Stafford bitch's second heat or oestrum is early enough to mate her. This condition, which is recognised by the vulva becoming enlarged and coloured, lasts between sixteen and twenty-one days, but the actual time when the bitch will be ready for mating cannot be estimated accurately. There are wide variations among bitches. A minority will accept a male any time after the seventh day, when the vulva becomes soft and loses some of its colour. The majority, however, are better disposed towards the attention of the stud dog from about the tenth to the fourteenth day after the onset of the oestrum. In a few cases the bitch must be mated in a very short space of time indeed, and in this event careful observation is essential. Reluctance to mate is generally manifested by the bitch keeping her tail firmly between her legs, and very often she will snarl and snap at her suitor. Positive signs are the lifting and curling of the tail and the movement of her rear towards the stud dog.

If a maiden bitch is being mated it is helpful if the stud is a seasoned campaigner, as in such cases events can often be left to take their natural course. I always prefer two people to be in attendance, however, to ensure that no injuries are sustained.

After the dog has effected entry and has made his first reflexive actions, he may need to be held in position for a few seconds while coition, or the tie, takes place. This occurs when the dog's penis swells in the vagina forming a 'knot' at the rear of the penis. The tie may be of relatively brief duration or may last as long as fifty minutes but gives proof that sperm have been deposited.

When either of the dogs is inexperienced, it is particularly necessary to have competent handlers present when the tie takes place. One should hold the bitch while the other should carefully manipulate the stud by first lifting one of his front feet over the bitch's back so that both rest on the ground. The appropriate rear leg should then be passed over the bitch's back thus turning the stud so that the dogs stand rear to rear. Each handler should control his own charge so that the dogs do not pull apart from each other and cause unnecessary damage.

Within a few days of mating it is advisable to worm the bitch with one of the proprietary preparations now available. Worms not only adversely affect the bitch during pregnancy but deprive the developing embryo of nutrients and transmit the parasites to the unborn foetus. During pregnancy extra attention should be paid to the bitch's diet, which, in addition to her normal balanced intake, should include extra supplies of calcium and vitamins B, C and D. Calcium, cod-liver oil and brewer's yeast tablets are simple and relatively cheap methods of achieving this.

I believe a bitch should take normal exercise during most of the pregnancy, but during the last two or three weeks extreme forms of exercise, which may cause the bitch to abort, should be avoided. Generally, however, the bitch has these matters firmly under her control and adjusts to suit the situation.

Although there is no real substitute for practical experience when supervising whelping, there are basic rules for the beginner. The gestation period is normally sixty-three days, although there are individual variations. (Appendix 4 gives the normal gestation periods.) A whelping box should be provided for the bitch at least a week before the litter is due to arrive so that she can familiarise herself with the whelping quarters. For a Stafford the whelping box should measure approximately 1m by 0.65m (3ft 6in by 2ft 6in), thus allowing sufficient space for the bitch and puppies; remember that it will also be used as a bed for the puppies for the following eight weeks.

The sides should be high enough to keep the puppies within, and a farrowing rail should be provided around three sides to prevent the occupants being damaged. It is convenient if the front is constructed with two removable sections; as the puppies become more mobile they can be allowed out of the box or kept within it as desired.

In adverse conditions young puppies can die from cold, and although Staffords are extremely hardy, it is advisable to suspend an infra-red lamp at an appropriate distance above the whelping box. Many breeders use newspaper as a base material during whelping, but others prefer old blankets or sheets, cut to size, and fastened to the floor of the box. Often the bitch tears up these coverings, but in any event they should be disposed of after whelping and fresh ones regularly provided.

The first signs that the bitch is about to whelp will be her restlessness, apparent discomfort and scratching in order to improve her position for comfortable delivery. There is then a 'pouting' of the vulva with an increased discharge, followed by straining and panting, which indicate that the birth of the first puppy is imminent.

At this stage the contractions can be both seen and felt. An opaque bag of membranes filled with fluid and containing the puppy should emerge from the vulva. It is preferable for the puppy to appear head downwards, as the bag will dilate the birth passage so that the body can follow easily at the next contraction. A 'breech' birth, where the puppy arrives tail first, may present greater difficulty, especially with large-headed puppies. If the head is near the orifice it can often be eased out during a contraction, but if this fails, a vet, previously informed of the impending litter, should be called.

The bitch will usually release the puppy from its membranes immediately after birth, but if it fails to do so, assistance must be given. The bag of membranes should be gently torn open so that the puppy can begin to breath. The puppy has been attached to the mother by an umbilical cord, and normally the bitch will bite through the cord and eat the placenta. If not the breeder will need to pinch the cord about 3cm (1½in) from the whelp's abdomen and cut the cord with sterilised scissors about the same distance from the umbilicus; the cord can then be tied with sterilised thread an inch or so from the navel.

It will be apparent that the presence of the bitch's owner is often necessary at whelping time, although many breeders prefer to remain in the background, on permanent 'call' if required. Much depends on the bitch, as some appear to appreciate their owner's permanent presence at this time.

After the birth of the first pup, the remainder of the litter should appear at intervals of between ten minutes and one hour; if two hours or more elapse, and the owner believes that whelping has not been completed then the services of a vet may be necessary. When it is established that the last puppy has been born, the bitch should be encouraged to leave the whelping box, to drink warm milk and glucose and to urinate. When she returns, all the puppies should feed and the bitch rest peacefully. At this stage the infra-red lamp should be switched on so that the puppies may be kept at the correct temperature.

It is seldom possible to overfeed a nursing bitch, which requires a protein-based diet supplemented by milk, cod-liver oil and extra vitamins and minerals in the form of Vetzyme and Stress.

As soon as the puppies are able to stand, no matter how insecurely, they can be taught to lap from a saucer or similar receptacle. The various baby-food preparations already mentioned are ideal to commence this operation, and this form of feeding will supplement the mother's milk. This is of greater importance, of course, if there are significantly more puppies than the Stafford's normal litter of four to six.

Introduction to solid food must be gradual but can take place from about the age of three weeks, starting with a thick milk mixture through a porridge type texture to the more advanced complete solids. From about the fourth week, breeders feeding proprietary 'complete' foods should follow the makers' instructions; those planning their own diets should begin to introduce scraps of fresh raw meat. For a Stafford these should be about the size of a table tennis ball and given twice each day.

As the puppies progress this amount can be gradually increased, until by the time they are due to leave their dam they should be taking about 120g (4oz) of minced raw meat twice a day plus a milk mixture baby food such as Farex in the same quantity. Obviously there are differences in the amounts individual puppies will consume at any age, and the progress of each member of the litter should be carefully monitored. As has been previously mentioned, the maxim of little and often is essential in rearing puppies. The onset of diarrhoea may indicate too much food or the wrong type of food; it can also be caused by an infection.

Puppies should be wormed at the age of three, five and seven weeks before they leave their dam at about eight weeks. In no circumstances should they be taken before this age.

7
EXHIBITING AND JUDGING

Sooner or later the majority of owners of pedigree dogs are attracted by the lure of the show-ring. Unfortunately there are a number of new exhibitors whose initial results fail to match up to their aspirations and who, unless they are given the correct advice and encouragement at this stage, are often lost to the show-ring forever. Conversely, there are many exhibitors who, despite failing to meet with immediate success, become more than ever determined to achieve it. Some of these exhibitors will become our future judges, and it is for this reason that I have included exhibiting and judging in the same chapter. The two activities are interdependent, and without them there is little doubt that the whole world of pedigree dogs would be much poorer, if indeed it continued to exist at all.

Any potential exhibitor should join his nearest specialist breed clubs and should certainly attend a number of shows as a spectator before entering the arena himself. We sometimes forget that a novice is often completely bewildered by the types of show and the criteria necessary for entry into the various classes. Although such information is invariably given in show schedules, the definition of classes is not always easily assimilated, and Appendix 5 therefore attempts to clarify the definitions so that beginners may be conversant with them before stepping into the show-ring. This information should, of course, be supplemented by frequent visits to shows and by discussions on all aspects of exhibition with experienced enthusiasts who will, in general, welcome the opportunity of sharing their knowledge. Having read Chapter 3 on the Breed Standard you should have a mental picture of the ideal Stafford; as perfection seldom exists it is soon realised that every specimen of the breed has some aspect of its anatomy which could be improved upon. Frequent attendances at championship and open shows, where some of the best Staffords in the country are being exhibited, will soon teach the novice exhibitor the main differences between what is and what is not required in the show-ring.

Fortunately the Staffordshire Bull Terrier is a breed which is relatively easily prepared for exhibition, unlike some other breeds which require regular stripping and trimming and, in the case of the long-coated varieties, constant attention. As the Stafford is a short-coated breed, it requires little preparation, assuming that the dog is in perfect physical health; this generally manifests itself in a short silky coat possessing a marked sheen. The appearance can be further improved by regular brushing and a final 'polish' with a piece of velvet or nylon.

Many exhibitors trim the long hairs off the underside and sides of the tail, using a variety of instruments to perform this task. I find that the task can be successfully accomplished with a sharp pair of scissors, but I would guard against clipping too much hair from the tail as this can give the appearance of a 'rat tail' which, to me, has less aesthetic appeal. If the dog is regularly exercised, and if at least part of this exercise is over hard ground, there should be little necessity to clip toe nails, but it is quite in order to do so and special clippers can be obtained for the task. It is certainly better to clip the toe nails than to enter the show-ring with an exhibit where they can be seen to have become overgrown.

Many exhibitors give little further attention to their dogs, although some, especially those with pied dogs or those with a fair amount of white markings, use chalk to enhance the appearance of their dogs. Anyone who has been benched next to a breed of dogs where chalking is not only usual but essential, will be aware of the problems associated with white chalk dust, although I must confess that I once owned a very good pied bitch on which I used a white chalk block when she appeared in the only four championship shows in which she was exhibited. The fact that she won two challenge certificates was coincidental! For some unaccountable reason, in general, owners of Staffordshire Bull Terriers appear to spend less time in training their dogs in show-ring deportment than do the owners of other breeds. Some enthusiasts would of course assert that this is more

'The First Cross' by Vero Shaw – probably examples of Bull and Terriers, early nineteenth century

Old English Terriers by Vero Shaw, early nineteenth century. One of the breeds involved in the evolution of the Staffordshire Bull Terrier

Rendorn The Mighty Quinn, owned and bred by Mr and Mrs N. Berry in 1976, another useful dog sired by Ch Hurricane of Judael

apparent than real, as Staffords, by their very nature and with their fighting background, are less tractable than other breeds when placed in the relatively confined area of a show-ring among other dogs. However, it is a matter to which all exhibitors should direct their attention, as it becomes quite impossible to assess the virtues and faults of any exhibit if it is constantly jumping at its owner or failing to walk in the ring in the manner prescribed by the judge.

Dogs should be trained to stand in the 'alert' position, especially when the judge is inspecting them, and to move freely, without straining at the lead, in order that movement can be correctly assessed. A good experienced judge can learn a great deal about a dog's anatomy from its movement, especially if he inspects it not only from the front and the rear, but also from the side. Indeed, it is only from the side that the stilted action, typical of the straight-stifled exhibit, can be easily seen.

Probably the best type of show for a first entry is the primary or limited show of the nearest Staffordshire Bull Terrier Breed Club. Secretaries of the breed clubs will be pleased to send schedules of their shows and, subject to any specific club rules, enrol potential exhibitors as members of their club. One doesn't need to be an exhibitor or breeder to join a club, but most societies require the nominee to be proposed and seconded by existing club members.

Primary shows are a relatively new innovation, which the Kennel Club approved from 1 July 1980. Such shows, which can only be held by breed clubs, are confined to a maximum of eight classes. The most 'advanced' class that can be included is a 'Maiden' class, and exhibits which have won a first prize at any show (Puppy, Special Puppy, Minor Puppy and Special Minor Puppy classes excepted) or a challenge certificate or a reserve challenge certificate may not compete.

An important feature of primary shows is that entries can be taken until the day of the show and no catalogues need to be printed. Breed clubs are to be allowed to hold up to four such events annually. Primary shows should prove very popular with both beginners and breed clubs because of their comparative informality, but, at the time of writing, there is insufficient evidence available to make an accurate estimate of their ultimate value.

For the beginner however, primary shows should afford an opportunity to enter a dog in a comparatively informal event with the minimum of expense. He will not be troubled by the need to despatch entries some time before a show is to be held, yet will presumably be able to obtain the opinion of a judge with a specialist knowledge of the breed. He will also have the opportunity to discuss the dogs with his fellow exhibitors, which is probably the best way to acquire knowledge of a breed, even if the advice, generously given, is not always accurate!

A typical limited show, which in the past has been the testing ground for beginners, may consist of fifteen classes, seven devoted to dogs, seven to bitches, together with a Veteran class for either dogs or bitches. The main advantage of a show of this type, organised by a specialist club, is that all the exhibits are Staffordshire Bull Terriers, the judge will in all probability be someone who has bred and exhibited specimens of the breed for many years, and facilities are available to enjoy the company of others who have similar interests with a similar breed of dog.

In such a typical show the classes may well be as follows:

Puppy   For dogs of six and not exceeding twelve calendar months of age on the day of the show.
Junior   For dogs of six and not exceeding eighteen calendar months of age on the day of the show.
Maiden   For dogs which have not won a first prize at any show. (Puppy, Minor Puppy and Special Minor Puppy classes excepted.)
Novice   For dogs which have not won three or more first prizes at any show or shows. (Puppy, Special Puppy, Minor Puppy and Special Minor Puppy excepted.)
Post-graduate   For dogs which have not won five or more first prizes at open or championship shows in Post-graduate, Minor Limit, Mid-limit, Limit or Open classes, whether restricted or not.
Limit   For dogs which have not won seven or more prizes in all at open or championship shows in Limit and Open classes, confined to the breed, whether restricted or not.
Open   For all dogs of the breed for which the class is provided and which are eligible for entry at the show.

A further seven classes of the type mentioned above would be devoted to bitches, and finally there would be a Veteran dog or bitch class for dogs of possibly seven years of age or over on the day of the show. The age of a veteran can be varied according to the definition of the class decided upon by the club holding the event but, according to Kennel Club regulations, must be a minimum of five years on the day of the show; it is more usual for six or seven years to be specified.

These classes are not, of course, completely comprehensive, and further information is given in Appendix 5. It should be noted that puppies under six calendar months of age are not eligible for exhibition at any show in this country, although puppies of under six months are eligible for exhibition in other countries in certain special events.

Having decided to enter his dog in a limited show, the beginner should write to the secretary or show secretary of the club concerned for the necessary schedule, which will set out complete information regarding the last date for entries, the date and time at which the show takes place, the name of the judge, the entry fees and the prize money to be allocated to the winners of the various classes. Included with the schedule will be an entry form requiring details of both the exhibitor and his dog. This information includes obvious things such as name and address, the registered Kennel Club name of the dog, its date of birth and the names of its sire and dam; all this information is required for inclusion in the catalogue of the show.

Entry form submitted, the beginner should present himself at the venue at least half an hour before the start of the show to familiarise himself and his exhibit with the environment. Shows are held in a wide variety of places, some excellent for the purpose, others unfortunately lacking certain amenities but representing the best that the club has been able to obtain in that particular area. The exhibitor should immediately obtain a catalogue, which will give a great deal of information including the sequence of classes; the exhibitor should study this so that he does not miss any of the classes for which his dog is entered. As a further safeguard the information is announced publicly by the ring steward before each class is judged.

THE NORTH EASTERN STAFFORDSHIRE
BULL TERRIER CLUB
Under Kennel Club Rules and Show Regulations

COMMUNITY CENTRE, EDEN LANE, PETERLEE

SPECIMEN
COPY ONLY

PLEASE USE
SEPARATE FORM
FOR EACH BREED
OR OWNER

Entries Close:

Entry Fees	
First Entry	60p per Dog
Subsequent entries	40p per Class

(On no account will entries be accepted without fees)

SATURDAY, 20TH SEPTEMBER, 1980 (POSTMARK)

INSTRUCTIONS This form must be used by one person only, (or partnership)   Writing MUST BE IN INK OR INDELIBLE PENCIL
Use one line only for each dog. The name of the dog and all the details as recorded with the Kennel Club must be given on this entry form. If an
error is made the dog may be disqualified by the Committee of the Kennel Club. All dogs must be REGISTERED at the Kennel Club and if a
Registered dog has changed ownership the TRANSFER must be registered before date of Show. A Puppy under 6 months old cannot be exhibited.
When entering more than one breed or variety, use if possible, a separate form for each. On no account will entries be accepted without fees.

REGISTERED NAME OF DOG	BREED	SEX D or B	Full Date of Birth	BREEDER	SIRE (BLOCK LETTERS)	DAM (BLOCK LETTERS)	To be entered in Classes numbered
ZENDIKS ZIRCON	STAFFORDSHIRE BULL TERRIER	B.	29.12.79	W.M. MORLEY	BODEGAS DANNY BOY OF ZENDIKS	ZENDIKS DYNAMITE	8.9.10
BODEGAS DANNY BOY OF ZENDIKS	-do-	D.	6.4.77	B. RICHARDSON	MOEKENS TORNADO	SNAPDRAGON OF KENSTAFF	7.
DENNYBECK DERRYGIRL	-do-	B.	22.7.69	MISS J. HORSFALL	DENNYBECK DEVIL MAY CARE	DENNYBECK BRINDIS PEPPER	15.

ONE LINE FOR EACH DOG, PUT CLASSES IN NUMERICAL ORDER & CHECK ALL DETAILS BEFORE POSTING

DECLARATION
I undertake to abide by the Rules and Regulations of the Kennel Club and of this Show and I declare that the dogs
entered have not suffered from or been knowingly exposed to the risk of distemper or any other infectious or
contagious disease during the six weeks prior to exhibition and I will not enter them if they incur such risks between
now and the day of the Show.

I declare that to the best of my knowledge the dogs are not liable to disqualification under Kennel Club
Show Regulations.

Usual Signature of Owner(s): ......W.Morley...... Date .....14.9.80......

Note: Dogs entered in breach of Kennel Club Show Regulations are liable to disqualification whether or not the
owner was aware of the breach.

BLOCK
LETTERS

Name of Owner(s) (MR) W.M. MORLEY

ADDRESS "GROVELANDS" RAINTON GROVE
HOUGHTON-LE-SPRING
TYNE & WEAR DH5 8NG

Telephone No. (0783) 842004

Entries and Fees which MUST BE PREPAID to be sent to: Show Secretary
MR. A. D. METCALFE,
29 CLEVELAND TERRACE,
DARLINGTON, CO. DURHAM.   Telephone: DARLINGTON 484695

It may be that the beginner has been able to acquire a good Stafford which does very well at the first show for which it is entered; it may be that, despite being a good specimen of the breed, the dog has met better competition on the day; or it may be that a fairly moderate specimen has done well because the rest of the class have been inferior specimens. The main thing is to remember that this is the assessment of one judge only; within the Breed Standard there is a great deal of discretion, and this is one of the reasons why your dog may win one week and not the next. The most important thing is that you should be aware of the virtues and faults of your own dog and, as your experience increases, be able to recognise the virtues and faults of other dogs. Unfortunately such knowledge can be gained only by many years of experience. It is true that some people have a natural talent for assessing a dog but enthusiasm and application are also necessary.

At this stage it may be of value to provide some very basic information which could prove helpful to newcomers to the show-ring. Although schedules and entry forms may present little difficulty to the experienced exhibitor, the beginner often makes errors in completing the entry form; a photostat copy of a completed entry form shows a specimen entry which is simple, easily legible and helpful to all show secretaries.

The variety of show-rings is nearly as great as the variety of breeds of dog. Many rings are too small, making it virtually impossible to assess movement; others have floors with surfaces that make even a Stafford unsure of its foothold. Sometimes the management is at fault, but often it is a case of obtaining the best available compromise when suitable premises are difficult to obtain.

At unbenched primary or limited shows, exhibitors are usually permitted to come and go as they wish, but if they do not respond to the steward's call when their class is due in the ring, they have no redress; a similar concession is now available at some championship shows.

Most championship show organisers provide exhibitors with information about car parks and directions for access to them. Unfortunately it is generally left to beginners to find out for themselves that a substantial chain is necessary when dogs are benched, that blankets or rugs are essential and that no respectable exhibitor travels to a show without a flaskful of hot tea or coffee. A suitable container for this miscellany of equipment not only ensures an ordered bench but may prevent pilfering.

Having arrived in good time and attuned himself to the atmosphere of the show, the exhibitor should now try to relax until the ring steward calls for dogs in his class to enter the ring. Entrance into the arena must be effected smartly but in as relaxed a fashion as possible, as owners must be careful not to transmit their own anxieties to their dogs. The steward will hand each exhibitor a number, which should be worn in a prominent place so that it can easily be seen by judges, stewards and spectators.

When you are summoned to the judge, proceed unhurriedly and 'set-up' your dog to its greatest advantage. Concentrate on your charge and endeavour to keep him fully alert, especially when the judge is looking at him. You will be asked to 'move' your dog, ideally in a triangular pattern, making full use of the ring, so that its movement can be assessed. Staffords, notoriously playful and boisterous, should be given adequate preparation for this exercise, as some judges become impatient when witnessing exhibits pulling their owners up and down the ring. Judges cannot assess movement under these conditions, and exhibitors cannot justifiably complain if their dogs are penalised. After making his decision in each class, the judge will line up the exhibits, usually from left to right, in order of merit. The ring steward will then call out the numbers of the winning dogs, and successful competitors will be handed their prize cards.

It is a breach of etiquette to speak to the judge, or indeed to other exhibitors, while judging is in progress; if you wish the judge to enlarge on his decisions, wait until proceedings have been completed.

If you don't win, remember there are other shows and other judges. We have all experienced the frustration of inferior exhibits beating our own, and should accept that judging dogs is a highly subjective matter.

Of all the topics discussed by dog fanciers of every breed there is little doubt that the alleged vagaries of judges and of judging is the most popular. Judges can expect to attract criticism each time they step into the show-ring, and most of them at some time in their judging careers will be castigated by some sections of exhibitors. It is evident that some judges will be more competent than others, but once inside the show-ring their decisions are unchallengeable, their word is law and there is no appeal. It has been said that even the ruling of a judge in a court of law is subject to appeal and that there should be avenues of appeal for disgruntled exhibitors. My own view is that we should keep our hobby in perspective and use the analogy of the football referee or the cricket umpire rather than that of the judiciary.

Sanctions are, of course, available to an exhibitor who feels that a judge has been incompetent or dishonest; he can simply refuse to enter future shows where that particular judge is officiating. Examples may be cited, however, of incompetent judges who, despite these sanctions, have continued to secure judging appointments year after year. It may be true that some appointments of judges tend to be made by popularity and patronage, but most are made on merit and experience; in any event it would be difficult to establish an alternative system which is close to perfection.

It may sound naive but I believe that the majority of judges are basically honest when giving their opinions in the show-ring. This is not to suggest that we should always agree completely with their verdicts. In the first place the Breed Standard is an imperfect document, at best allowing a range of interpretation and at worst being completely ambiguous. In addition, the Standard, along with the Standards of other breeds, allows for a high degree of subjectivity, which all of us, despite our claims to the contrary, indulge in periodically. It is, for example, a widely held, if untrue, belief that 'all-round' judges are more concerned with general soundness than their 'specialist' colleagues, who are supposed to devote much more attention to 'fancier's points'. (A 'specialist' is a judge who officiates purely at shows devoted to one breed whereas the 'all-rounder' is a judge who deals with a variety of breeds.) In recent years the 'specialist' has become more popular than the 'all-rounder' and this trend will probably continue within the breed, despite the inherent dangers.

We should be aware that there are wide differences in the amount of knowledge possessed even among our best judges. For instance, the choice of championship show judges is based partly on expertise and experience, but it has also been described as a pure popularity poll, and there are some who claim that there is some substance in this allegation. There is, therefore, a wide divergence in the ability of judges, although it is probably true that the very worst of them are self-destructive. It should be emphasised that the Kennel Club, the ruling body for the activities of all pedigree dogs in the United Kingdom, ratifies the appointment of championship show judges before they can judge this type of show.

Finally, although I have mentioned that I believe that most judges are basically honest in their placings, it often happens that their assessments may be conditioned by external influences. This manifests itself in a 'follow-my-leader' syndrome; a respected judge awards a challenge certificate to a certain dog, and a number of other judges feel that it may be impolitic to disagree. Thus, when we consider that judges, besides possessing different degrees of knowledge and being differently affected by external influences, have also to contend with a Standard that contains ambiguities, it is inevitable that inconsistencies will result.

What is the alternative to all this? Let us suppose we lived in a perfect world where the content of the Breed Standard was crystal clear, where judges were completely informed and infallible and where each exhibit was presented in the same impeccable condition. Dog showing would surely be reduced to a clinical examination with the same exhibits winning each week and all the anticipation and excitement removed from our hobby. Perhaps after all the present methods, with all their faults, are preferable even if they are in need of modification.

8
SPORTING ASPECTS

Although the name Staffordshire Bull Terrier was not commonly used to distinguish the breed until about 1935, there seems little doubt that the Bull and Terrier of the later part of the nineteenth century was not dissimilar to some of those dogs which collectively formed the basis of the breed in 1935. In the Black Country the breed was known as the Bull and Terrier or simply as the 'Stafford', a diminutive of the present official title which today is commonly used. In other parts of the country the breed was referred to as the 'Pit Dog' or the 'Fighting Terrier'. By whatever name it was known, the dog was associated with many sports that are today illegal and would be considered by many to be barbarous. Paintings and engravings from the nineteenth century depict scenes of a wide variety of sporting activities including bull baiting, bear baiting, badger baiting, dog fighting and rat killing. As bull baiting became illegal in 1835 some present-day accounts of these activities may be apocryphal, but there are at least some witnesses of badger baiting and of organised dog fighting alive today who could narrate some blood-curdling stories if they so wished.

The Protection of Animals Act of 1911 finally made organised dog fighting and animal baiting illegal. (The relevant sections of the Act are given in Appendix 6.) There is some evidence, however, that these sports still exist in certain parts of the British Isles, and periodically there is a public outcry, often sensationalised by the media, against such activities. However, the vast majority of present-day Staffordshire Bull Terrier owners have never seen organised dog fighting; most would find it appalling. Probably all of them can admire fighting dogs, but they would not wish to participate in organised dog fighting. It seems that many of our ancestors were ambivalent in their approach to dog fighting. The majority appear to have had a genuine affection for their dogs, yet they were capable of committing them to the dog pit with the possibility of death and the near-certainty of injury.

Forms of bear baiting are reputed to have been practised as long ago as Roman times, and there is evidence of its popularity in England from Norman times until towards the end of the eighteenth century. Bear gardens, as the bear-baiting areas were called, were either privately owned by noblemen and landed gentry or provided by commercial entrepreneurs for popular amusement. An example of this latter type was London's famous Bankside, a riverside thoroughfare on the south bank of the Thames between Southwark and Blackfriars Bridges and the site of an Elizabethan pleasure resort, where theatres, taverns and brothels flourished alongside bear baiting and bull baiting. Here the charges were 'a penny for admission, a penny at the entry of the scaffold [stage] and a penny for quiet standing'. The sport consisted at that time of tethering a bear to a wall or central stake in such a manner that it had a limited circumferential range; in order to make the risks more acceptable to the attackers, the 'sportsmen' of the day occasionally blinded the bear before the baiting began. The unfortunate animal was then beaten with staves and set upon by dogs, which were of course the 'bull dogs' of that period.

Mary Tudor and Elizabeth I were both supposed to be supporters of bear baiting, and in 1591 the Privy Council ordered that all theatres should be closed on Thursdays, as this was the day bear baiting generally took place. Apparently the royal personage did not wish proceedings to be diluted by competitive entertainments! Sunday also appeared to be a favoured day for the sport, this being the only day of the week when most working men were granted any leisure time. The churches campaigned strongly against what would now be considered to be inhuman social outrages, and bear baiting, along with bull baiting, was finally abolished by Act of Parliament in 1835.

It is possible that the ancestors of the present Staffordshire Bull Terrier were involved in bear baiting towards the end of this period, but the dogs used would in general have been much larger than our present-day species, probably more like the bull dog of the era and almost certainly weighing over 50lb.

Bear baiting appears to have been popular in the United States of America until much later into the nineteenth century, and there it was common practice for bears and their keepers to have a somewhat itinerant role. Many gruesome stories are recorded, although it is not generally possible to vouch for their authenticity. One such incident reputedly took place outside an Army barracks in Canada about 1840. An American, complete with bear and dogs, had informed the Army officers that he was prepared to provide an entertainment for them – no doubt at a price – in the form of a bear bait. When the travelling dogs proved to be no match for the bear, the commanding officer of the unit sent for his bull bitch in the hope that she could improve on the efforts of the other dogs. Meanwhile the bear's owner had lengthened the tethering chain of the bear to give it greater mobility, with the result that the bitch, placed at some disadvantage, suffered a broken leg and two fractured ribs. She was quickly withdrawn from the battle and taken to the Army doctor who placed the damaged bones in splints and supplied the bitch with a bed in the medical quarters.

Later that evening the officers were having dinner when their meal was interrupted by a soldier who had been despatched from the medical quarters to the mess room to inform the commanding officer that the bitch had escaped from its convalescent sanctuary. Despite its injuries it had jumped from a window of the medical room, hobbled to the bear's cage and in that confined area had attacked and choked the bear, which was later found dead by its irate owner. The messroom message was that the bear's owner was now chasing the bitch in a violent fashion, bludgeon in hand, attempting to wreak his own revenge.

Although parts of this anecdote may test one's credulity, there are many who can vouch for the tremendous tenacity and imperviousness to pain of the Staffordshire Bull Terrier. I once saw a young bitch struck by a double-decker bus, which seemed to be travelling at about 25 mph. She was caught by the nearside front wheel and flung a distance of no less than 10ft onto the pavement. The bitch, which suffered quite severe injuries including a broken leg and broken ribs, did not even emit a howl of pain and was able to walk to her home some two hundred yards away. This Stafford is now eleven years old, suffers from a painful arthritic condition caused by the injuries, yet remains cheerful and still allows young children to take the most outrageous liberties with her.

Although the involvement of the Staffordshire Bull Terrier in bear baiting is not certain, it is known that it was heavily involved with bull baiting; indeed this sport was the origin of the very existence of the breed. Bull baiting probably originated at the beginning of the thirteenth century, and, although it co-existed with bear baiting for some years, it soon became the more popular sport; by the beginning of the fourteenth century many towns throughout Britain had their own bullring. As with bear baiting, bull baiting was occasionally accorded royal patronage and by the seventeenth century it was a popular sport with noblemen and the landed gentry.

Originally the bulls were probably running free in a confined area, but later the bull was tethered to a stake, and the object of the exercise was for the dogs to take hold of the animal, usually by the nose, and retain a grip for as long as possible. Some writers suggest that the bull dog of that era, while having courage, tenacity and strength in abundance, lacked the agility to evade the bull in such a confined situation. Others suggest that a smaller dog, approaching his adversary by crawling along the ground, was less likely to be gored by the bull's horns.

Whatever the reason, at about the beginning of the nineteenth century bulldogs were crossed with terriers to produce the Bull and Terrier already described as the ancestor of our present Staffordshire Bull Terrier. I repeat that I am not certain that the terrier used was necessarily the Old English Terrier; the term 'terrier' was possibly a generic one applied to any terrier-type dog and a wide variety of such animals may have been used in the original cross-breeding.

Some sickening tales are told about bull baiting, which, if true, would make a modern Spanish bullfight look a relatively humane sport. Although the dogs were gored, tossed and often seriously injured, the poor bull seldom got respite as yet another dog would be let loose to attack as soon as its predecessor had been disposed of by the bull. Eventually the exhausted bull, tongue hanging from his mouth, would be set upon by yet another dog, with the end result that his tongue was either badly lacerated or torn out altogether. Fortunately the sport, if it can be so called, did not appear to have lasted long after the turn of the century and, of course, was abolished completely by Act of Parliament in 1835.

With the passing of bull baiting, owners of Bull and Terriers directed their attention towards dog fighting as a substitute. Dog pits became popular in many parts of Britain, although the main areas of interest appear to have been Staffordshire, London and, to a lesser degree, an area south of the Tyne in north-east England. As a native of the north-east I am unable to find a satisfactory explanation for the last-mentioned venue. It may have arisen from the industrial connections between the chain-making areas of Staffordshire and shipbuilding activities of Tyne and Wear.

Although there are many different theories about the rules of dog fighting which regulated contests during most of the nineteenth century, there appears to be agreement that they were carefully framed documents which were generally honoured by the various owners of the protagonists. The commonest theory is that there were articles of agreement, together with seventeen rules, and that they were virtually unchanged during the whole period of legal organised dog fighting. Copies of the articles of agreement and of the rules are given below.

Rules of Dog Fighting

ARTICLES OF AGREEMENT made on the __ day of __ 19__.
_____ agrees to fight his _____
dog _____ pounds weight, against _____
_____ dog _____ pounds weight, for £____
aside at _____ on the _____ day of
_____ 19__. The dogs to be weighed at _____
o'clock in the _____ and fight between _____ o'clock
in the _____.

The deposits to be made as in hereinafter mentioned; to be delivered
to _____ (who is the final Stakeholder),
namely, the First Deposit of £_____ aside at the making of the
match; the Second Deposit of £_____ aside, on the _____ of
_____ at the house of _____ : Third Deposit
of £_____ on the _____ of _____ at the
house of _____: Fourth Deposit of £_____
on the _____ of _____ at the house of
_____ and the Fifth Deposit of £_____ on
the _____ of _____ at the house of
_____ which is the last.

RULES

1st   To be a fair fight   yards from the scratch.

2nd   Both dogs to be tasted before and after fighting if required.

3rd   Both dogs to be shewn fair to the scratch, and washed at their
own corners.

4th   Both seconds to deliver the dogs fair from the corner, and not
leave until the dogs commence fighting.

5th   A referee to be chosen in the pit; one minute time to be allowed
for sponging; and at the expiration of that time the timekeeper shall
call 'make ready', and as soon as the minute is expired the dogs to be
delivered, and the dog refusing or stopping on the way to be the loser.

6th   Should either second pick his dog up in a mistake, he shall put it
down immediately, by order of the referee or the money to be forfeited.

7th   Should anything pernicious be found on either dog, before or
after fighting in the pit, the backers of the dog so found to forfeit, and
the person holding the battle money to give it up immediately, when
called upon to do so.

8th   Referee to be chosen in the pit before fighting, whose decision in
all cases shall be final.

9th   Either dog exceeding the stipulated weight, on the day of
weighing, to forfeit the money deposited.

10th   In any case of a dog being declared dead by the referee, the
living dog shall remain at him for ten minutes when he shall be taken
to his corner if it be his turn to scratch, or if it be the dead dog's turn
the fight shall be at an end by order of the referee.

11th   In any case of police interference the referee to name the next
place and time of fighting, on the same day if possible and day by day
until it be decided, but if no referee be chosen, or goes away after being
disturbed, then the power of choosing the time and place of fighting to
be left with the stakeholder and a fresh referee to be chosen in the pit,
and the power of the former one to be entirely gone.

12th In case of police interference and the dogs have commenced fighting they will not be required to weigh any more, but if they have not commenced fighting they will have to weigh day by day at   lb until decided at the time and place named by the referee, or if he refuses or goes away then the stakeholder has to name the time and place.

13th The seconder of either dog is upon no consideration to call his adversary's dog by name while in the pit, nor use anything whatever in his hands with which to call his dog.

14th To toss up the night before fighting for the place of fighting, between the hours of   and   o'clock at the house where the last deposit was made.

15th The above stakes are not to be given up until fairly won or lost by a fight, unless either party break the above agreement.

16th All deposits to be made between the hours of   and   o'clock at night.

17th Either party not following up or breaking the above agreements, to forfeit the money down.

_____
_____
_____
_____
_____

WITNESSES _____ SIGNED_____
_____   _____

In the United States, although the general substance of the rules was similar, they were even more complex and specified for example that the pit should be 16ft square with sides 2ft 6in high, a wooden floor and an apparently more sophisticated type of line demarcation. It seems also that different parts of the country favoured different-sized pits and although most were square, a circular pit was also used. In England most of the old prints and drawings suggest that the pits were either square or rectangular but there appears to have been no specific regulation size. Whatever the ring was like, a white 'scratch line' was drawn across the centre, and at either end of the pit was a 'corner' to which the dogs were taken during temporary lulls in a fight.

American Dog Fighting Rules

WHEREAS It is the aim of the United Kennel Club Registering Office, its members, and the Pit Bull Terrier Fraternity, to place 'Pit Contests' upon a recognised plane of excellence and promote more and better contests, the following rules have been adopted by the Fraternity and the United Kennel Club Registering Offices.

One Pit contests to be recognised must employ a UKC licensed referee.

Two The Principals may select any licensed UKC referee in good standing.

Three The principals may select any fancier for the official timekeeper, but such selection must meet with the approval of the referee.

Four A licensed referee shall not preside over any 'Pit Contest' where one or both of the combat dogs are non-UKC registered 'Cur' bloodlines.

Five The combat dogs must be UKC registered in their rightful owners' names and the referee shall make sure of this and be in possession of their Registration Certificates during the contest.

Six The referee shall deliver to the United Kennel Club Registering Offices a full and complete report of the contest within five (5) days after the contest.

Seven Any dog winning three (3) moneyed contests held under these rules and presided over by a UKC licensed referee, shall have the degree of Champion conferred upon him by the United Kennel Club Registering Offices and the Pit Bull Terrier Fraternity.

Eight It shall be the duty of the official timekeeper to keep a correct record of the time consumed in the contest by scratch, and the number of scratches, etc, and he shall deliver the original time sheet (or a duplicate) to the referee immediately after the contest to be sent to the United Kennel Club Registering Offices for record. It shall also be the duty of the official timekeeper to call to the referee before the scratch twenty-five (25) seconds 'Get Ready', and thirty (30) seconds 'Let Go', and the referee shall act accordingly.

Nine The full amount of the contest money shall be in the hands of the final stake holder before the referee orders the dogs weighed. The referee shall order the dogs weighed one (1) hour before the contest and they shall be weighed in the presence of the referee and the final stake holder and either dog exceeding the weight specified in the agreement shall forfeit then and there to his opponent all money posted.

Ten After weighing the dogs the referee shall toss a coin for the principals and the principal winning the toss shall have his choice of

Jenny the Rocker with her puppies by Winterfold Danny which were bred by Mrs M. Briscoe (*Animal Photography Ltd*)

Bodegas Danny Boy of Zendiks, Best in Show winner, line bred to Ch Benext Beau. A good example of strength and agility, essential Stafford characteristics

Ch Hurricane of Judael, photographed with his owner Eddie Pringle, Chairman of the Breed Council. This dog, bred in 1974 by the successful partnership of M. Searle and G. Earle, has already sired seven UK champions

having his dog washed (first or last) also his choice of corner in the 'Pit'.

Eleven   Each principal shall furnish a sponge and two towels for washing and drying his opponent's dog. Both dogs shall be washed in the centre of the 'Pit' with warm water and washing soda. Fifteen (15) minutes shall be allowed each principal to wash his opponent's dog. The time between washing each dog shall not exceed five (5) minutes and the washing of both dogs thirty-five (35) minutes.

Twelve   After washing and drying, each dog shall be placed in the hands of a watchful fancier in the corner of the 'Pit' selected or assigned to him and kept there until the principals are given the word 'Let Go' by the referee. Each principal shall 'let go' his opponent's dog at the start and thereafter shall handle his own dog.

Thirteen   There shall be only one container of water in the 'Pit' for sponging between a 'pick up' and a 'scratch' and each principal shall furnish a sponge and two towels for sponging and drying his dog. The referee shall examine the sponges and water and have full charge of them at all times.

Fourteen   It shall be a fair 'scratch in turn' contest. Thirty (30) seconds shall be allowed between every 'pick up' and 'scratch', twenty-five (25) seconds for sponging, drying and fanning, and five (5) seconds to get ready.

Fifteen   To establish a fair 'turn' which will entitle either principal to 'pick up', both dogs must be free from holds and the dog which is accused of 'turning' must have turned his head and shoulders from his opponent. Either principal upon noticing this action may appeal to the referee and claim the 'Turn' and if the claim be just and fair the referee shall immediately call a 'pick up' and notify the other principal it is his turn to scratch.

Sixteen   At twenty-five (25) seconds the referee shall call 'get ready' and at thirty (30) seconds he shall call 'let go' and the principal of the dog to scratch shall take his hands off his dog fair inside of his 'scratch line' and to be a fair 'scratch' his dog must go across the 'Pit' inside his opponent's 'scratch line' and mouth his opponent. Should the dog fail to go across and mouth his opponent he loses the contest and the referee shall immediately announce the winner.

Seventeen   While one dog is 'scratching', the opponent shall hold his dog's head and shoulders fair between his legs just inside his 'scratch line'.

Eighteen   Should a dog while 'scratching' become confused and sway to either side of a direct line to his opponent as long as he does not turn his head away from his opponent he is making a fair 'scratch'.

Nineteen   Should any outsider attract the dog's attention while 'scratching' and the dog stop, or 'scratch' the article or object instead of his opponent, the referee shall immediately order the dog 'Scratched' over.

Twenty   Should either dog become fanged, the referee shall order a 'pick up' and allow the principal to unfang his dog, then immediately order them put down two feet apart and give the word 'let go'. This action does not have any connection with a 'Turn' or 'Scratch' and must not be considered so. Principals can unfang their dogs with their hands without picking them up if the referee so decides.

Twenty-one   Should a fair 'Turn and Pick Up' be made and the dogs accidentally get in hold again, the referee shall order them parted and proceed in thirty (30) seconds with the 'scratch'.

Twenty-two   Principals shall be allowed to encourage their dogs by voice and actions. Should a principal touch either dog with his hand, foot or other article while in action the referee shall immediately call a foul and announce his opponent the winner.

Twenty-three   Principals shall take their hands off their dog fair inside their 'scratch line'. Should a principal push his dog over his 'scratch line' the referee shall immediately call a foul and announce his opponent the winner.

Twenty-four   Should a principal pick his dog up without being told to by the referee, the referee shall immediately call a foul and announce his opponent the winner.

Twenty-five   Should a principal leave his corner before the dogs have resumed action, the referee shall immediately call a foul and announce his opponent the winner.

Twenty-six   Under no circumstances where a match is made and money posted, shall the money be returned without a contest. The principal appearing for the contest shall be declared the winner and receive the 'stake' money.

Twenty-seven   Should interference of any kind prevent a fair decisive contest, the principals and the referee shall name the next time and place for the contest (within fifteen (15) days.) Should the principals and the referee fail to agree upon the future meeting place, it shall then be the duty of the referee to name the time and place and the same referee shall preside over this unfinished contest and the principals and referee shall start this contest with 'Rule 3'.

Twenty-eight   Any person or persons found guilty of doping, faking, poisoning or attempting to dope, fake, poison or damage any dog or dogs, before, during or after the contest, shall forfeit all money, be fined $100 and be barred from the Pit Bull Terrier Fraternity for a period of three (3) years, and a full report of such action shall be printed two times each year for a period of three (3) years in the June and December issues of the United Kennel Club Journal *Bloodlines*.

Twenty-nine   In all recognized contests the decisions of the UKC licensed referee shall be final and all bets shall go as the 'main stakes'.

Thirty The 'Pit' shall be 16ft square with sides two and one half feet high, with a tight wood floor. A line shall be painted across the centre, also a scratch line painted across each principal's corner. To draw this scratch line, measure 7 feet out each way from the corner.

Thirty-one These rules may be amended or altered by a two-thirds vote of the Fraternity at any meeting of the Fraternity, providing notice of such amendments or alterations and their nature has been given the Fraternity at least thirty (30) days previous to such meeting and such alterations and amendments must meet with the approval of the Fraternity which are Members of the United Kennel Club Registering offices, before they shall be adopted.

Dimensions of the Dog Pit

Circular pit Twenty-four feet round, eight feet in diameter, thirty inches high, when the boards are straight.

Square pit Eight feet square, thirty-six inches high, with a border of three and one-half inches wide, of Virginia pine; the boards grooved. Fourteen feet square with sides two feet high.

The study of the terminology of organised dog fighting is fascinating; much of it derives from the world of boxing, and many of the words and phrases in common use today, therefore, have their origins in the dog pit. Although boxing probably originated as long ago as Roman times, when it was a gladiatorial spectacle, it is in England that the 'noble art' was really developed. The first boxing booth was opened in London at the beginning of the eighteenth century and from about the middle of that century to about 1820 there was tremendous support for the sport. During this period boxing appeared to straddle a wide spectrum of social class and it is interesting that the names of many well-known boxers of that period were eventually used as the names of Staffordshire Bull Terriers later in the nineteenth century. Gentleman Jackson, who made a fortune out of his pugilistic activities, and Tom Cribb seem to' have been remembered by later Staffordshire Bull Terrier enthusiasts. It is perhaps not surprising that those eventually attracted to keeping fighting dogs should also have had an interest in pugilism. Readers will have noted that the terms 'corner' and 'sponging' appear in the rules, words commonly used in boxing circles today. Referees and stakeholders are not of course confined to boxing terminology, but it is interesting to note that these terms are used in dog-fighting rules. 'Throwing in the towel', however, when the owner of a dog feared that his charge might be losing the day, is specific to boxing.

As will be observed from the articles of agreement for a British dog fight, the weights of the contestants, like the weights of modern-day boxers, were of supreme importance. The tolerance allowed was minimal, and it was rare for contestants to be more than one or two pounds different. Rule 2, relating to the 'tasting' of dogs before and after fighting, allowed an examination of the dog's coat to ensure that no dressing had been applied to it which would place its opponent at a disadvantage. The usual procedure was for the 'taster' to use milk and a towel to wash and then wipe the whole of the opposing dog's coat in order to obviate any chance of an illegal dressing having been applied. I find it difficult to believe, as some observers maintain, that a person physically licked the entire body of the dog with his tongue to ensure that no obnoxious substance had been added to the coat. My experience of real fighting Staffords – not in any organised way I hasten to add – is that in the heat of battle no pernicious dressing, however distasteful, would deter them from their task. Readers who have experienced the difficulty of separating fighting Staffords will know what I mean. I am not of course referring to reports of modern organised dog fighting, in America where, it is alleged, nicotine sulphide has been applied to dogs' coats resulting in the partial paralysis of opponents.

The referee, chosen in the pit, was responsible for officiating and the contest was started by the timekeeper calling 'make ready' or 'get ready'; if one of the dogs refused to advance towards his adversary, stopped on the way or failed to cross the scratch line he was the loser. 'Not coming up to scratch', a phrase in common use today, derives from the dog pit. Other terms in common usage today include 'top dog' and 'bottom dog', phrases used to describe the position of the dog in a fight: obviously the top dog was the one getting the better of the fight. A 'fast dog' was generally quarrelsome, out of control – and cowardly! He was seldom a game dog, usually made a lot of noise and beat a hasty retreat after a short duration. The phrase is still occasionally used in certain parts of the country to mean the same thing. It has also been suggested that 'fast and loose' may have had its origin in the breed, although that is perhaps stretching the imagination. Presumably 'loose' in this context would mean 'not tethered'; you can draw your own conclusions from this!

Gruesome tales are recorded of organised dog fights. A strange one described an incident when a handler brought his dog to scratch where it 'toed the line' – and died. However its opponent failed to come to the scratch line and the dead dog was declared the winner.

The dog-fighting fraternity of the nineteenth century attached less importance to looks or genetic theory in their breeding programmes than to mating winner to winner. Success in the pit seemed to be the only criterion and if some form of line breeding resulted it was purely coincidental. Strangely, supporters of dog fighting did not appear to think that their sport was particularly brutal or barbarous. Their philosophy appears to have been that if a challenge was made and accepted by protagonists of equal weight, it was perfectly acceptable. Most Stafford owners today would find this philosophy abhorrent. For anyone interested, however, a detailed account of a fight is given in the next chapter.

The badger, an attractive animal which has been romanticised by many writers, is the subject of numerous anecdotes relating to sporting dogs. Certainly the Bull and Terrier appears to have been used to a great extent for badger baiting, and although not as highly organised as dog fighting there are records of badger-baiting rules. Apparently the unfortunate animal was placed in a badger box about 8ft long, 2ft high and 1ft wide, closed at one end. The object of the exercise was for the dog to enter the box and to draw the badger's head to the open end of the box within a specified time. If the dog succeeded it counted as a 'draw', if not a failure. As with all the nineteenth-century blood sports, wagers were made on the various dogs, and perhaps the betting aspects were a primary motivation.

The badger is, of course, a tough animal, and it would take a good dog – even a Stafford – to master one. There are those who, in their eagerness to preserve the species, claim that badgers are entirely herbivorous in their habits. This is not so; like the human, they are in fact omnivorous, and will eat young birds and poultry and indeed seem to relish rabbits. Having made the point, however, I would not like to see the species endangered, and the reduction in keepers on our country estates has reprieved the badgers who might have met their final demise in such unpleasant pieces of mechanism as gin-traps. Before the last war a number of country people were involved in badger-digging; this is different from badger baiting, as the badger was in no way confined to the badger box and could often escape. Although no accurate figures are available, it has been suggested that the total badger population was diminishing annually because of these digs, and fatalities mounted to several thousand each year throughout the country. Badger digging, unlike badger baiting which was made illegal in 1911, can still be undertaken in certain circumstances in accordance with the Badger Act 1973 which makes it an offence for a badger to be killed, injured or taken except by authorised persons; in my experience landowners and farmers become involved only when a rogue badger may be depleting their poultry stock. Indeed the present intensive systems of poultry keeping are usually a safeguard against marauding animals, be they badgers or foxes, and there is no need whatever to kill badgers — except of course in the Ministry of Agriculture's gassing campaign in areas where badgers are thought to carry bovine tuberculosis. Nevertheless there have been reports of increased illegal badger digging and some conservationists have expressed great concern.

Many owners of today's Staffordshire Bull Terriers may never have seen a live badger face to face, and would be surprised by the toughness of the skin, the size of the teeth and of the mouth; although it has the reputation of being a friendly and playful animal it obviously has the ability to defend itself against most aggressors.

The first time I came in close contact with a badger was in unfortunate circumstances. I was driving one of the first Minis down a dark country lane one evening at about 60 m.p.h., when a low, black and white apparition fleetingly caught my attention and in a second there was the most resounding thud as my vehicle ground to a halt. As I emerged I could see that a large boar badger had run across the road right in the path of my car; the unfortunate animal had been killed instantly. I had of course read of badger baiting because of my interest in Staffordshire Bull Terriers. As I gazed on this sizeable boar weighing probably 18.12k (40lb), with tremendously powerful jaw and huge mouth, I soon realised it would take a very game dog indeed to tackle such a creature in a frontal attack.

Finally among the so-called organised sports with the breed was that of rat killing. Even this, when indulged in on an organised basis, was the subject of wagers, which were again probably the major attraction. Here the rules appear to be flexible, but in general there was a relationship between the weight of the dog and the number of rats to be killed in a given time. The rats were placed in a circular pit from which there was no escape; when the dog entered it was required to kill all the rodents there. The dog killing the greatest number of rats in the shortest time, with whatever weight penalty incurred, was the winner. In some cases a rat catcher was recruited to bring live rats to the pit, but occasionally the owner of each of the protagonists was required to bring along the necessary number of rats. One has visions of some of the owners of dogs of that period spending as much time breeding giant killer rats as in perfecting their canine stock!

Although I have not been involved in organised rat killing I recall an incident shortly after I bought my first Stafford, a very light bitch of terrier dimensions quite unsuitable for the show-ring. The local rodent officer had suggested to me that a Stafford was too large and ungainly to be an effective rat killer, and that what was required was a smaller type of terrier of much lighter build and, in his view, greater agility. One evening he arrived at my home with a cage containing four live rats, a number which no doubt the 'old-timers' would have thought to be derisory for a real rat-killing Stafford. As my dog had never ever seen a rat before I was not happy at the suggestion that the rats should be freed from their captivity in my vegetable garden. I eventually agreed to the suggestion however and had obviously been overanxious, for within ten seconds not one live rat remained. Perhaps some of our heavier specimens today may not be as competent, but I have never yet owned a Stafford that would not kill rats.

In view of existing legislation, readers may wonder what sporting activities exist today and what opportunities are available to test the determination, endurance and tenacity of their dogs. Some owners still illegally involve themselves in badger digs — and some of their dogs have the scars to prove it! Others claim that their charges are able to catch rabbits and other small game. Most Staffords, despite their great substance, have an astonishing turn of speed for 55–75m (60–80yd), although I find it difficult to believe the claim that they are as fast as whippets over this distance! Some years ago a friend who bred whippets used to bring to our kennels a dog that would play with my bitches in an adjoining pasture. Much as I would like to report that my dogs were able to make circles around the whippet, the truth is that on most occasions they were at the rear of the field!

Recently however I was judging at an open show in Scotland organised by the West of Scotland Terrier Club. At least once each year the members of this club enjoy organised terrier racing, which is based on the old type of whippet racing. A rabbit skin or other form of lure is attached to a rope which is wrapped around a drum attached to a bicycle wheel, hand-propelled by the usual arrangement of sprockets and chain. There are of course various methods, but the general idea is that the competitors at a set starting point are released to chase the lure, which is pulled by the cycle mechanism at an appropriate speed in the direction of the finishing line. This particular club presents a quite sophisticated event, with the dogs placed in traps at the starting line and released by mechanical means. Of course in some forms of whippet racing the handlers 'slip' their dogs at the start and a good getaway requires a good handler.

Obviously it would be unfair to match a small-legged terrier such as a Border with a dog as large as an Airedale; to redress this imbalance there are usually three classes, for small, medium-sized and large terriers. The distance run is usually 73m (80yd), which suits the Staffordshire Bull Terrier very well indeed. Club officials inform me that a Stafford was a consistent winner of the medium-sized terrier class. To add greater interest, steeplechase events are occasionally staged by placing bales of straw across the entire course at strategic intervals. Staffords also do well here as they are able to negotiate two or three bales of straw as easily as David Hemery could negotiate high hurdles!

Before concluding this chapter I should perhaps sound a slight note of warning to readers who have not yet been fortunate enough to own a Stafford, but are contemplating purchasing one. Like all breeds there are individual differences, but in general most Staffordshire Bull Terriers will fight – some only when the occasion demands, others more frequently. Some training is essential and can partly compensate for the possible peccadilloes of your dog in this respect – but perhaps not entirely. In certain circumstances even the best-trained dogs find the attraction of combat too great to resist. Always keep your charge on a lead on public roads or where traffic exists, or you will almost certainly regret it sooner or later.

No intelligent owner looks for a fight but incidents may occur; don't be alarmed if they do. No matter what the size of opposition it is unlikely that your dog will be in real trouble – unless the opposition is also a Stafford! However, protagonists must be separated as quickly as possible, and to do so requires some elementary knowledge. Your dog will probably have hold of his opponent by the throat, but you should resist the desire immediately to involve yourself by attempting to pull your dog away. On the contrary you should attempt to take up an astride position over your dog, and 'lock' his hind quarters between your knees, thus reducing his mobility. Rather than pulling you should attempt to push your dog towards his opponent at the same time twisting his collar in an attempt to put pressure on the windpipe. If this is effected successfully he will relinquish his hold in order to obtain the supply of oxygen needed to continue the fight. If this is successful then you can pull him away, ensuring that the other dog does not take hold in the process. Only experience makes for real competence and two knowledgeable people will always accomplish the task more easily than one! Although your dog will never purposely bite you, it is unwise to allow your hands near the 'sharp' end of his mouth during the excitement of combat; your fingers will certainly be in danger if they stray in the direction of the opposing dog's throat.

Finally I tell a cautionary tale of an incident which happened quite recently. We own two bitches, now veterans of eleven years, who have been raised together since they were puppies; for reasons irrelevant in the context of this story, neither has had a litter. They have been kennelled together most of their lives, taken part in the same activities and apparently formed an excellent canine relationship. Although they have been involved in fights with other dogs, they have only occasionally had brief skirmishes with each other, altercations which were promptly settled. One evening my wife had offered the facilities of our home for a whist drive in aid of a local charity. Normally the two bitches are allowed inside each evening from about 5pm, but at about 7pm that evening, when the function began, they were to be banished to their kennels as one of the visitors was allergic to dogs. Earlier in the evening my wife had unknowingly dropped a loaf of bread outside the house when she had been bringing in supplies for the evening's refreshments. The red bitch, who would not normally eat bread offered to her, had apparently seized the loaf and hidden it near the entrance to the kennel run.

Having been assigned the task of returning the dogs to their kennel on the arrival of the allergic lady, I called for them but they appeared somewhat reluctant to be disturbed from their normal routine. However they eventually left the house and walked, somewhat sullenly, into the darkness of the area surrounding the kennels. Within seconds I heard a cacophonous commotion and perceived that on passing the loaf of bread the red bitch, which had hidden it, had suddenly launched herself on to her brindle companion. The brindle had reciprocated and both had good holds! Although reasonably experienced in separating fighting Staffords I was astonished by the ferocity exhibited by both bitches until they – and I – were quite exhausted; indeed I can seldom recall greater difficulty in separating two dogs. The sequel is that they have lived together in perfect harmony ever since.

Perhaps the moral of the story is that fighting can sometimes erupt without apparent provocation, and Stafford owners must always be aware that this is the case. Such incidents may never happen of course, and potential owners should not be deterred by such possibilities. As all Stafford owners will tell you, the attributes of the breed more than compensate for their occasional indiscretions.

9

ORGANISED DOG FIGHTING

Although the Staffordshire Bull Terrier may have had its origins in a Bull and Terrier conceived for a specialised form of bull baiting, it was dog fighting which was responsible for the growth in the popularity of the breed during the nineteenth century. For this reason, no matter how abhorrent dog fighting may be to readers, any book on the breed would be incomplete without an account of an actual dog fight. Although few, if any, of today's owners would contemplate involving themselves in organised dog fighting, the position was quite different during the nineteenth century and early years of the twentieth century. Captain Lawrence Fitz-Barnard in his book *Fighting Sports*, originally published as late as 1920, attempted to justify dog fighting:

> Dog fighting is not generally practised, and for the reason that the dog is such a faithful, loving friend that one hates to see him hurt. The reason is rotten, and worse than rotten; one does not let a brave animal fight to save one's own feelings. The dog loves a fight, but as usual we think only of ourselves.

This is an opinion to which the vast majority of us would never subscribe.

Since dog fighting has been illegal in this country for many years it is not possible to obtain a living eyewitness account of a legally organised dog fight. There are however blow-by-blow accounts of such fights by sporting writers of the nineteenth century, notably Pierce Egan, a well-known journalist of that era. More recent accounts of dog fighting in the United States of America are given in *The American Pit Bull Terrier* by Joseph L. Colby, originally published in 1936, and also in the American journal *Bloodlines*, the official publication of the United Kennel Club Incorporated, which was being published as late as

December 1940. The magazine, published in Kalamazoo, Michigan, contained graphic accounts of organised dog fights, challenges from one owner to another and even an advertisement assuring readers that 'Merck's phosphate of calcium fed to a bitch during oestrum was guaranteed to produce 75 per cent male puppies in each litter!' Perhaps the authenticity of the account of the dog fights came into the same category as the magazine's medicinal claims!

With some reluctance I have however attempted to reconstruct an organised dog fight which took place in the famous – or infamous – London's Duck Lane, in the first half of the nineteenth century. Sensitive readers should perhaps omit this part of the book and concentrate on those chapters dealing with selection, management and exhibition.

The fight took place one Thursday evening between a London dog known as Attila, whose owner presumably knew about the activities of Attila the Hun, and a little-known outsider, reputedly from Staffordshire, named Belcher, after Jem Belcher, a well-known pugilist of the period. Attila was a black brindle dog over five years old weighing 33lb, known in Duck Lane for his past exploits. He had been victorious in nine previous fights, in four of which he had actually killed his opponent; truly an aptly named dog!

The Staffordshire dog was younger, weighing 32lb, and was something of an unknown quantity. He was a red pied dog, about three years old. There also seemed a dearth of information about his owner and handler Charlie Grew, apart from the fact that Charlie had originated from Staffordshire and was known to be an 'iron man'; whether this term referred to his occupation or to his physical and temperamental qualities is not known. The contest attracted great public attention, and so many local fanciers supported the event that the venue was filled to overflowing and many would-be spectators found difficulty in viewing the proceedings. The arena was illuminated by a multitude of candles held in an immense glass chandelier located over the centre of the pit.

At 8.00pm, the preliminary arrangements completed, the dogs were brought into the pit, Belcher by his owner, who was also doubling up as a second, and Attila by Mick Purcell, an experienced London handler, who was to be responsible for the dog's conduct in the pit. The dogs were taken by their respective seconds to opposite corners of the pit, each marked with a chalk line and containing water and sponges, with an assistant outside the ring as a bottle holder. A referee and timekeeper had already been chosen from the ringside and agreed upon by representatives of the two opposing camps. The scene was set for the commencement of battle and the ringside reverberated with the customary comments of the 'expert' spectators.

'That Staffordshire dog looks too light and all pieds are a bit cowardly.'

'Attila's getting on a bit now, he may be past it.'

'Did you see what he did to that red dog two months ago?'

'He's a dirty fighter too – always goes for the privates.'

Round 1

The ringside chatter continued until the dogs, now firmly ensconced in their seconds' hands, were turned away from each other at extreme angles of the ring and the warning 'make ready' was given. Suddenly there was complete silence; five seconds later the command 'let go' was given and the two dogs threw themselves at each other, meeting at the centre of the pit with a grinding crunch as their jaws interlocked in their struggle for mastery. Neither dog would give way; minutes seemed to elapse as they stood anchored on the same spot, their heads engaged in combat, swaying in deadly motion. Attila, confident from previous victories, appeared well composed, but Belcher, with Charlie Grew on his knees, verbally fondling his charge, seemed unconcerned by the situation. Suddenly Attila, sensing he had a tough opponent to deal with, moved back, broke and then, with head to ground, attempted to get between the pied dog's forelegs to effect his own destructive work. Belcher seemed to sense Charlie's signal and turning quickly around took hold of the brindle's neck keeping his jaws in motion in an attempt to obtain a better hold.

Now it was Mick Purcell who was encouraging his dog, and a desperate rally ensued that lasted several minutes until both dogs seemed unable to move. At this juncture Belcher appeared to turn away, and Charlie quickly grasped his charge and clasped him to his chest, thus ending a most desperate round.

Round 2

During the minute's interval both dogs were rapidly washed in their respective corners, and it was the turn of Belcher, looking remarkably refreshed, to meet the enemy. He flew to the scratch line but Attila was completely prepared and immediately took a cheek hold. Belcher effected disengagement and again both dogs were in the centre of the ring plunging, pulling and hauling. It was becoming evident that Attila was fighting with cunning while Belcher relied mainly on agility and perpetual motion.

Eventually the pied dog got his opponent down but even while he lay on the ground Attila kept his teeth at work on his opponent's throat. However, the older dog now seemed to be the first to show lack of wind, and his panting indicated some distress. Suddenly, with a super-canine effort, Attila reversed the positions, became top dog and nailed Belcher to the floor grasping his throat so effectively that the poor animal's mouth opened, his tongue lolled out and he appeared to be in dire distress.

In these exchanges fortunes were changing rapidly, and now it was Belcher on top although both dogs appeared to be near exhaustion. Attila lay panting on his side, and Belcher, with his tongue still out, was standing over him, being urged by Charlie Grew to punish Attila to such an extent that the dog would be unable to come to scratch in the next round. Experienced Mick Purcell was fully aware of the situation however, and as soon as the pied dog turned away he picked up his dog to end the round.

Round 3

Attila was ready in time to start the round and approached the scratch line with his usual venom. At this stage the black brindle looked to be the stronger and, despite being foiled in his own attempt at foul fighting, his opponent was also suffering badly.

If Attila's lungs had been sound enough to have enabled him to sustain the onslaught, it could well have been the end of Belcher, but both dogs were now feeling the strain, and having fought to a standstill were now simply staring at each other from opposite sides of the pit.

Round 4

During the minute interval the odds on Attila had lengthened from evens to 6–4, although few of the London spectators believed that he was losing the battle.

Belcher, suitably refreshed after Charlie Grew's administrations, raced to the scratch line with renewed vigour, but Attila had also found reserves of energy; nonetheless the strength was now ebbing from both dogs. Again the black brindle attempted his usual ploy but Belcher was now wise to the situation. After this sharp rally both animals lay down panting, Belcher turned away and the round ended.

Rounds 5–10

From this stage to the tenth and final round there was little variety in the fight. The energy had visibly deserted both dogs but especially Attila whose advancing years were now constituting a great handicap. Often on his back as the under-dog, he saved himself from further punishment by making the maximum use of his front paws, which kept his opponent from acquiring a neck hold. Victory now depended on the art of persuading the appropriate dog to reach the scratch line on time being called; to fail to do so would be to forfeit the fight. All the mysteries of the art were practised by each second in refreshing his dog, rousing him at the scratch, starting him from it and by violent stamping at the psychological moment impelling him forward even though the dog was able to perform inadequately after he had reached the scratch line. Belcher, game to the last, went in with great spirit, and poor Attila fought with wonderful resolution until the last round when his legs failed him and nature refused to bear him to the scratch; he received great acclamation from the assembled spectators. Thus ended his long career of victories, and the red pied dog was the hero of the day. The winner was carried around the pit in triumph and poor Attila was removed to receive the medical ministrations of his owners. Attila was subsequently retired from dog fighting and

'The Dog Fight' by Henry Alken, 1824, showing Bull and Terriers in a fairly typical dog pit

'The Bulldog' by W. L. Smith – mid-nineteenth-century print depicting an ancestor of the Staffordshire Bull Terrier

Staffordshire Bull Terriers can be allowed to play safely with young children

Ch Pitbul Red Regent, owned and bred by Ken Fensom in 1975. Best of Breed at the 1980 Windsor Championship Show

lived to a ripe old age; nothing further was heard of the activities of the very game and powerful Belcher. Both he and his owner vanished ethereally into the night.

If this account of a nineteenth-century dog fight has not made pleasant reading perhaps it will give further resolve to those of us who are determined finally to terminate such gruesome spectacles.

10

THE CONTEMPORARY SCENE

When it is considered that the first Staffordshire Bull Terrier was registered at the Kennel Club less than fifty years ago, most would concede that, by any canine standards, tremendous progress has been made. There is now a degree of uniformity among many specimens of the breed; thirty years ago it was occasionally difficult to recognise some of our registered stock as Staffords! There are, of course, no grounds for complacency, as a dramatic increase in the numbers of any breed of dog attracts associated problems. When we obtained our first Staffordshire Bull Terrier in 1948, a fairly typical puppy could be purchased for a quite nominal amount; today some typical specimens are realising high prices. Even allowing for inflation, the cost in real terms appears to have at least trebled.

Fortunately I have seen little evidence as yet of breeders producing puppies purely for profit or of dealers becoming extensively involved with the breed, but I am informed that such things are happening in certain parts of the country, and it would be unfortunate for the breed if such activities were to escalate. My own feeling is that the very nature and temperament of the breed is such that it is not really suitable for large-scale breeding operations; this may be its salvation. As mentioned previously, I consider that Staffords possess the greatest amount of 'humanism' of any breed of dog, and this, together with their fighting propensities, may deter the 'commercial breeders'; I hope so. Few Stafford breeders keep more than two or three brood bitches, and this also deters commercialism.

During the past forty years many breeders and exhibitors have inevitably disappeared from the scene, many new ones have arrived, and a rapidly diminishing few of the early breeder-exhibitors remain. During my early years in the breed I was fortunate enough to meet a number of original members of the

Staffordshire Bull Terrier Club, all of whom I knew are sadly now dead. There were some tremendous characters amongst them, but perhaps in thirty years' time, the enthusiasts of 2010 will consider that many of the exhibitors circulating around the benches in 1980 were themselves characters!

Previous chapters have dealt with the early history of the breed, but it may perhaps be of interest to examine in more detail the events of the past thirty years or so. This period not only includes the general growth in popularity of Staffordshire Bull Terriers and the consequent increase in the number of breed clubs, but leads to an examination of the people who have helped to make this possible.

The 'line and family system', so carefully and accurately introduced by the late H. N. Beilby and published in 1948, in his revised edition of *The Staffordshire Bull Terrier*, referred to six main lines of dogs in the breed and to over forty families of bitches, which were constantly added to by Mr Beilby until his untimely death in April 1954.

I corresponded regularly with Mr Beilby while I was Breed Correspondent to *The Dog Fancier*, and still have in my possession many letters and records that illustrate how carefully he researched his information. From this correspondence we were able to trace the ancestry of many Staffords in addition to our bitch which was later to produce the north-east's first champion, and to which Family Number 64 was eventually allocated by Mr Beilby.

It would require a complete treatise to deal adequately with the subject, as the breed has developed to such an extent that many of today's enthusiasts may find difficulty in locating the lines and families of their current stock. The 'M' line, so named as its originator in modern records was a dog called Brindle Mick, has perhaps distinguished itself more than the others in the quantity of stock produced. Champion Gentleman Jim, a striking pied dog, sired by Brindle Mick out of Triton Judy, was clearly one of the best dogs of his day and probably the most prolific sire in this line. Many of the best dogs of today can be traced back to Ch Gentleman Jim, although the 'M' line does not of course have the monopoly of fine Staffords.

For the benefit of newcomers to the breed, the other five lines, with their originators in modern records, are the 'J' line (Fearless Joe), the 'L' line founded by Game Lad, the 'R' line (Ribchester Bob), the 'B' line, so called because Rum Bottle was its founder, and finally the 'C' line (Cinderbank Beauty). The 'C' line was originally referred to as the 'T' line, but Mr Beilby felt that the 'C' line would be more appropriate as, in his view, its founder was Cinderbank Beauty.

Owners of today's Staffords, unless they delve back many generations, are unlikely to find the names of these dogs in their pedigrees, but by a little research it is not difficult to trace a particular dog's ancestry, and it is of course an absorbing task, especially if one is able to relate the names in the pedigrees to any photographs that may be available of dogs of that time. In this connection, an occasional magazine, published privately by Fred Phillips of Stourton, could be of use as it contains a profusion of photographs of past and present Staffordshire Bull Terriers.

Initially it seemed that the 'J' line would assume the greatest importance, for it produced two extremely good dogs which were to have an influence on the breed, Vindictive Monty and Jim the Dandy. Jim the Dandy, a dark brindle dog, which has been mentioned in earlier chapters, sired some good dogs which contributed to this particular line, including Tackle, Emden Convoy, Chestonian Security and Chestonian Overdraft.

The 'L' line's founder, Game Lad, produced Champion Game Laddie and Our Ben; other early dogs in this line were Brinstock Democrat and Brigands Bashem which appeared regularly in some early pedigrees. The 'L' line is of interest, not only because it produced Ch Game Laddie, one of the earliest champions, but because the breeder and owner of this dog, W. A. Boylan, contributed so much to the early development of the breed. Mr Boylan, who retired to Suffolk some years ago, is one of the few survivors of the breed's early enthusiasts and can be considered to be 'Mr "L" line', for he owned its originator, Game Lad. Game Lad, whelped in December 1929, six years before the birth of the first Staffordshire Bull Terrier Club, was by Bilston Bill out of Sedgely Queen, both, of course, dogs unregistered with the Kennel Club.

Game Lad was the type of dog from which our present-day specimens have developed. Higher on the leg, and showing a greater bias towards terrier than bulldog, I must confess that Game Lad and his son Ch Game Laddie appeared more efficient fighting machines than many dogs at present in our show-rings.

Ch Game Laddie was born in January 1936, and was by Game Lad out of Mad Molly. Mr Boylan bred many good dogs, including another early bitch Ch Madcap Mischief and a superb bitch Ch Brinstock Sandy Bridget, both by Ch Game Laddie.

The most prominent dogs in the 'R' line were perhaps Ribchester Max and Vindictive Monty of Wyncroft, along with Milkern Guardsman and International Champion Head Lad of Villmar, which was owned by the late Ron Servat of the Vancroft prefix.

The 'B' and 'C' lines do not perhaps figure as prominently in the earlier pedigrees but, when tracing the history of dogs, it is possible that in the 'B' line you may find Rum Bottle and Eager Lad, two of the line's early successes, and in the 'C' line, Togo and Pink Lane Spitfire.

Some breeders aver that families of bitches are more important than lines of dogs, and certainly there is some evidence that a few bitches have played a significant part in the evolution of numerous breeds of dog. However, as Mr Beilby eventually identified over sixty families of bitches, and was constantly adding to them, it is outside the scope of this publication adequately to deal with the matter. For those enthusiasts who wish to learn more of the early dogs, reference should be made to the 1948 edition of Mr Beilby's book *The Staffordshire Bull Terrier*, although copies may now be difficult to locate.

As dogs are able during their lifetime to produce many more progeny than bitches, some breeders often appear to put an emphasis on stud dogs. It must not be forgotten that both parents are equally important in any union but unfortunately some of our best bitches have not attracted the publicity, or the acclaim, of our best stud dogs.

Some of the early bitches which were responsible for producing today's families were unregistered in the early 1930s and some of the most successful dams of later years did not themselves gain top honours in the show-ring.

Although examination of the early lines and families is of more than academic interest to modern breeders, it is perhaps most important to have practical knowledge of strains produced by individual breeders. A number of successful breeders have established strains that consistently produce typical sound stock of similar appearance; this is, of course, the ultimate aim. It is quite legitimate to use the expertise and experience of other enthusiasts in this respect by a careful study of breeding programmes and a resolution not to repeat previous errors.

Unfortunately there is no magic recipe for instant success, but already some relatively recent entrants to the breed have succeeded in establishing useful strains in less than ten years. A combination of diligence and enthusiasm with an essence of luck can accelerate the process.

Since the first breed club was established in 1935 it has been joined by other specialist clubs extending throughout the British Isles, and there are now fifteen recognised breed clubs operating successfully. A full list of these clubs together with the names and addresses of the individual secretaries is given in Appendix 2.

There are two clubs in Scotland, both of which cover very large areas, one for the whole of Northern Ireland and twelve for England. All except the Northern Counties Staffordshire Bull Terrier Club and the North West Staffordshire Bull Terrier Club are in association by virtue of their membership of the Staffordshire Bull Terrier Breed Council of Great Britain and Northern Ireland. Although this Council has no real executive power and its decisions are not legally binding on constituent breed clubs, it plays an important role in the affairs of Staffordshire Bull Terriers, and its views are often sought by the Kennel Club and other important canine organisations.

The objects of the Council are to coordinate the activities of the breed clubs and generally promote Staffordshire Bull Terriers by whatever means possible. Meetings of the Council, which are held bi-annually, are often quite intense in both interest and participation, and in my view aptly reflect the

Stafford temperament. The present chairman is Eddie Pringle, mentioned later in this chapter, and the secretary is Mrs E. Nicolls, who is also treasurer of the Southern Counties Staffordshire Bull Terrier Society. The Constitution of the Council allows it to extend associate membership to all overseas Staffordshire Bull Terrier Clubs. One of the principal functions of the Council is to compile a list of judges who, in the view of the majority of clubs represented, are capable of awarding challenge certificates in the breed. In addition, each individual breed club compiles its own list of judges.

Although some of the previously mentioned specialist breed clubs have been in existence for many years, others have been formed as the breed has increased in popularity. Some areas, like my native north-east, were, for historical reasons, among the latest additions. In the north-east there was a combined Staffordshire Bull Terrier and Bull Terrier Club formed just after the last war, and such clubs were considered by the Kennel Club to be *general* canine societies since they catered for more than one breed. As may be imagined, insurmountable problems arose from this arrangement, especially when a judge, who was specialist in only one of the two breeds, was appointed to judge both breeds at club shows. It was not until 1976 that the position was rationalised and the newly formed North Eastern Staffordshire Bull Terrier Club held its first annual general meeting as a specialist breed club in January 1977.

One of the earliest enthusiasts in the north-east to achieve general success at championship shows was Joe Johnson of Fatfield, who had a small kennel of better than average Staffords. My own association with the club began in 1948, and I was fortunate enough to breed the first champion in the north-east in December 1950, a tiger brindle bitch, Champion Red Biddy of Zendiks out of my CC winning bitch October Lady of Zendiks by Mr Johnson's Brian's Choice. Red Biddy eventually matured into a fine bitch at the age of two and a half years, and gained her three CCs in 1953 within a short period of four months under the ownership of Dr J. Silveira. She eventually departed these shores when her owner moved to Canada. Shortly after our successes with October Lady and Red Biddy, our own breeding and exhibiting activities had to be curtailed, and our role in the north-east was taken over by the now well-known Rellim Kennels owned by Mr and Mrs J. Miller, who are certainly the most successful exhibitors so far in this area. Among their imposing list of champions was Ch Rellim A'boy and his son Ch Ferryvale Victor, one of the country's most successful sires. Since his wife's tragic death John Miller has carried on with the kennel in a more limited way, devoting more of his time, as we all seem to do as we advance in years, to the administrative and judicial aspects of the breed.

At present the most successful breeders in the north-east and arguably some of the most successful in the entire country are Mr and Mrs Ken Brown of the Moekens Kennels in the village of Lingdale in Cleveland. They have produced Crufts winners two years in succession, succeeded in breeding two champions in one litter and bred the Dog C.C. Winner at Crufts in 1978; more importantly however, they have been successful after a relatively short time in producing sound stock of similar type. Other successful exhibitors in the north-east are Jack Dunn of Dawdon, Alan Bloomfield of Cramlington, Mr and Mrs Brian Whitehouse of Hutton Sessay and, more recently, Glynn Carter of Middlesbrough with Ch Skean Dhu featured on the cover of this book.

Another relatively new breed club, and geographically one of our most remote, is the North of Scotland Staffordshire Bull Terrier Club, some of whose members have to travel over 150 miles to the nearest championship show. The club was formed in December 1970 with Dr A. Anderson of Old Meldrum, Aberdeenshire as secretary and J. Jeffrey of Aberdeen as chairman. It is interesting to record that in 1980 these two offices were both occupied by the same incumbents, and Dr Anderson in fact has fulfilled the role of secretary for the whole of this period without a break.

I recall corresponding with Dr Anderson nearly thirty years ago when I was Breed Correspondent of the *Dog Fancier*, and today, as then, she writes the most accurate, impartial and detailed accounts of the Stafford events in the north of Scotland. It is due entirely to the dedication of such enthusiasts as Dr

Anderson that the breed has become so firmly established in that part of the British Isles, for, when she first entered medical practice in Aberdeen, the whole town boasted only two Staffords.

Apart from Dr Anderson, whose well-known Bourtie prefix has been associated with numerous CC and reserve CC winners, many other fanciers from the north of Scotland have already made their mark in the breed and are determined to do even better.

Many Scottish fanciers are, of course, members of both the North of Scotland Club and the Scottish Staffordshire Bull Terrier Club, which, in general, has the remainder of Scotland in its catchment area. Over the years one of the best known and most successful breeders has been A. W. Harkness of the Senkrah prefix, whose quality bitches have produced many winners in the breed, and Mr and Mrs I. Dunn, who have produced some excellent dogs bearing their Durward prefix. More latterly Mrs Jean Short of Cranhill, Glasgow has been successful with her well-proportioned tiger brindle dog Ch Mac Schiehallion, which has been campaigned fearlessly throughout the country.

In Wales and the surrounding English districts there is also some duality of membership between the Western Staffordshire Bull Terrier Society, which was fortunate to have H. Jones of Ponthir as secretary until his tragic death early in 1980, and the Staffordshire Bull Terrier Club of Wales, where the enthusiastic S. A. Rumble of Rhondda holds the secretarial reins. The Welsh Club, formed in 1975, with the acquiescence of the Western Society has strong support among its members and is influencing the breed throughout Wales.

The Western Staffordshire Bull Terrier Society was formed in 1966 and originally wished to be known as the Wales and the West Staffordshire Bull Terrier Society to reflect its wide area of membership, but this title was not acceptable to the Kennel Club. The original pressure for the club's formation came from Jim Parsons (Tinkinswood) and Alan Mitchell (Hoplite), supported by the late Mrs Doris Hughes-Williams of the Linksbury prefix. With the help of its efficient and diligent first secretary, the late Major Frank Rowley, and assisted by an enthusiastic band of Welsh and West Country breeders and exhibitors, the society made rapid progress and now has a membership of approximately five hundred, covering a wide area, although it conceded a great deal of its territory to the Staffordshire Bull Terrier Club of Wales when that club was formed in 1975.

To the credit of the Western Society, its members unselfishly agreed to the formation of the Welsh Club, realising that the more remote Welsh valleys could not be adequately covered by the existing Western Society. Even so, many of the Western Staffordshire Bull Terrier Society's members find it necessary to travel for up to four hours to attend committee meetings, which are held in Bristol. The original chairman of the club was Jim Parsons, and the present chairman is Alan Mitchell; perhaps it is more than coincidental that these two members were instrumental in forming the society.

The present secretary of the Western Club is Mrs Pat Painter, and Jim Parsons still finds time, among his many commitments, to act as vice-chairman. This club is also unique in producing a year book and four newsletters annually in order to inform its widely scattered membership of what is happening not only in the club but in the world of Staffords. The newsletter is edited and produced by Mrs June Fisher who, together with her husband, operates the Flagstaff Kennels.

Not surprisingly the greatest concentration of Breed Clubs is in the area from which the Stafford originated. Besides the parent club, the Staffordshire Bull Terrier Club, whose history could command a book of its own and whose present secretary is N. Wootton, there are the Potteries Staffordshire Bull Terrier Club with the formidable L. F. Hemstock as secretary, and the Notts and Derby Staffordshire Bull Terrier Club with B. Grattridge at present responsible for its administration. Not far away is the East Midlands Staffordshire Bull Terrier Club, whose secretary John Monks has worked hard for the breed not only in his own region but also nationally.

On the east coast the experienced Mrs Joyce Shorrock, of the Eastaff prefix, has for many years helped to guide the fortunes of the East Anglian Staffordshire Bull Terrier Club, while in the west are the old-established North Western Staffordshire Bull Terrier Club and the relatively newly formed Merseyside Staffordshire Bull Terrier Club.

Another northern club with an enviable record of achievements is the Northern Counties Staffordshire Bull Terrier Club, which was formed as early as 1943, but by far the largest to date is the Southern Counties Staffordshire Bull Terrier Society, which covers a large slice of southern England, much of it of an urban nature, and which consequently has the largest population of any breed club in its catchment area. There are those who feel that this club is too large, and attempts have recently been made to form other breed clubs within its area. So far these attempts have been unsuccessful, and it is a matter of debate whether a club can wield too much influence. No doubt democracy will prevail and an equitable solution will be finally reached.

This club has always been fortunate in possessing enthusiastic and articulate officers who have undertaken some useful pioneer work for the breed, even if at times the club has felt the need to take unilateral action on some issues. This club's magazine, *The Stafford*, the official organ of the society, was inaugurated at the beginning of 1948 and is arguably one of the best produced specialist publications dealing with Staffordshire Bull Terriers. One of those most responsible for its success was A. W. A. Cairns, its first editor, whose interesting, if sometimes controversial comments, made it compulsive reading for many Stafford enthusiasts. There have, of course, been some excellent editors since Mr Cairns' departure from the editorial chair, and I feel sure that Mrs Roma Williams, the present editor, who along with her husband has devoted so much effort to the success of the publication, will continue to produce the magazine to the standard of previous editions. A more recent magazine is *The Stafford Bulletin*, published by the North Eastern SBTC.

Finally, the Northern Ireland Staffordshire Bull Terrier Club which, because of its geographical position, poses several problems to its members who have to cross the Irish Sea for all of their championship show events, apart from that held in Belfast, continues to survive and flourish.

Probably one of the most difficult tasks when producing a book on the Stafford is to make a selection of those contemporary dogs and bitches which have made a substantial contribution to the Breed; even the word 'contemporary' is capable of ambiguity!

Perhaps most would agree that any book on the Stafford without the mention of Champion Gentleman Jim, the breed's first dog champion, owned by the late Joe Mallen, would be singularly inappropriate. This well-known pied dog was taller at the withers than today's Standard allows, but nevertheless he was an outstanding specimen of his day. More importantly, he was not only a prolific sire but produced many good quality dogs, which have had a significant effect on the breed. If a selection had to be made of one dog only which had influenced the Breed more than any other the choice must fall on Champion Gentleman Jim. Among the many excellent dogs and bitches he produced which formed a firm base for the breed's development, Ch Gentleman Jim sired four champions, three dogs and one bitch. He accomplished this although, since he was born in May 1937, the war seriously interfered with the show careers of many of his progeny and no champions were crowned between 1940 and 1946. It was therefore a remarkable achievement, as only four champions gained their status during 1947, six in 1948.

Of the three dog champions produced by Ch Gentleman Jim — Widneyland Kim, Jim's Double of Wychbury and Fearless Red of Bandits — by far the most successful sire was Widneyland Kim, a dark brindle dog of classic outline, which sired eight champions, five dogs and three bitches. Ch Widneyland Kim, born on 8 March 1944, was bred by H. Harris and later sold to G. A. Dudley, whose Wychbury Kennels were associated with a number of champions, especially between 1946 and 1953. Probably the most successful of Widneyland Kim's progeny was Champion Wychbury Kimbo, owned and bred by Mr Dudley, which produced four champions himself; Kimbo was a strongly built fawn dog which gained early success in the show-ring.

Another of the earlier sires to make his mark was Champion Brigands Bosun, which produced three champions, one dog and two bitches. Bosun did not become a champion himself until he was nearly six years old. Not all the most successful sires of the early days of the breed were themselves champions. Jolly Roger, a grandson of Ch Gentleman Jim, sired four champions, all dogs, the best known of which were probably Champion Emden Corsican and Champion Quiz of Wyncroft. Another early dog which failed himself to achieve championship status but which sired dog champions was Bomber Command, a 'J' line dog sired by The Great Bomber, a well-built fawn dog with an excellent head.

Somewhat later in the 1950s a striking little pied dog, Champion Wychbury Diamond King, born on 13 August 1951, quickly achieved success and was crowned a champion in 1952. This dog, which was owned although not bred by Gerald Dudley, was also a successful sire, being responsible for two dog champions and one bitch champion during his stud career. Other successful sires of the 1950s were Champion Goldwyn's Leading Lad and Champion Bellerophon Billy Boy, and in the 1960s came Champion Major in Command of Wychbury and the prolific Champion Rellim Ferryvale Victor, which sired three champion dogs and two champion bitches.

Without doubt however, the outstanding sire so far in the recent history of the breed has been Champion Eastaff Danom, a dog born on 7 August 1955 and bred by Mrs J. Shorrock (nee Brightmore), sired by Champion Goldwyn's Leading Lad out of Champion Linda of Killyglen. This dog himself sired eleven champions in all, five dogs and six bitches, and it seems doubtful whether this record will ever be equalled in the breed.

During the 1970s a larger number of dogs shared the honour of producing champions, including Champion Topcroft Toreador, which sired seven champions, five dogs and two bitches; Champion Rapparee Rothersyke Vow, which produced five champions, three dogs and two bitches; the uncrowned dog Dennybeck Hard Diamond, which sired two champion dogs and two champion bitches; and Dumbriton Baldie Thompson, which sired three champions, one dog and two bitches. Champion Hurricane of Judael, owned by Mr and Mrs Eddie Pringle, is still only six years old at the time of writing, and he has already sired five UK champions with the probability of more to come; he poses the only current threat to the record of Eastaff Danom.

It has been said that any kennel is only as strong as its bitches. The selection of a stud dog is less complex than the selection of a brood bitch as the progeny of several bitches served by one stud dog can be evaluated, whereas in the case of a bitch, who may only produce three or four litters during her breeding life, the task is much more difficult. For this reason the breeder who is able to develop a family of bitches consistently producing like stock of high quality has a great advantage. It is therefore of prime importance for the beginner to identify such families and endeavour to acquire a brood bitch from such high quality stock if he is to contemplate breeding.

While it has been the exception rather than the rule for bitches to produce a number of champions during breeding operations, there have been a number of examples. A. W. Harkness seems to have been consistent in this respect and has owned a number of good quality bitches; probably the most successful was Senkrah Sabelle, which produced four bitch champions three of which were in the same litter by Champion Weycombe Dandy; born on 26 December 1960, they were Champions Senkrah Saffron, Senkrah Sapphire and Senkrah Sabeau. Senkrah Saffron herself produced two champions, a dog and a bitch, and it is this sort of family breeding that establishes worthwhile strains.

Another breeder who has achieved excellent results with his bitches is G. R. Down. In the late 1950s and early 1960s he achieved some notable successes, none more than with his home-bred bitch Champion Weycombe Cherry, born on 10 March 1954, out of Weycombe Jule and sired by Gentleman Jackson. On 30 June 1956 Weycombe Cherry gave birth to a litter which included three champions one dog and two bitches.

In more recent years, Mr and Mrs A. A. Waters of the Southern Counties Staffordshire Bull Terrier Society produced a home-bred bitch on 18 April 1968 which was to become Champion Ashstock Artful Bess. Apart from her successful show career, Artful Bess produced two litters in successive years each containing two champions. The 1971 litter contained two dog puppies, which were eventually to become champions, and the 1972 litter produced a dog and a bitch champion.

Not all successful brood bitches are, of course, themselves champions or need necessarily have pursued tremendously successful show careers themselves. There are genetic reasons for this, and readers wishing to study the subject should refer to a specialist book on genotypes and phenotypes. One such bitch in recent years was Swinfen Sunflower, a bitch owned by Mr and Mrs K. Brown, which produced some excellent stock including two champions in the same litter in 1974; indeed if one examines the list of champions in Appendix 7 of this book, it will be found that the vast majority of champions, whether dogs or bitches, emanated from dams who themselves failed to achieve championship status.

Before leaving the contemporary scene, mention should be made of current trends and attitudes. There is no doubt that in recent years the breed has captured the public imagination, and a number of supporters of other breeds of dog have been attracted to our ranks. The dangers of exploitation exist, and if the breed is to retain its 'naturalness', breeders and exhibitors must be aware of the problems which have been a contributory factor in lessening the original appeal in some other breeds of dog. A united front should be presented against any unsound features appearing in the breed such as undershot mouths, straight stifles and weak backs, and the magnificent temperament of the breed should be closely guarded. It should never be forgotten that our banner should always be able to be seen to be flying proudly carrying the key words of 'Strength and Agility', interwoven perhaps with a large letter 'T' for temperament.

11

THE AMERICAN SCENE

Staffordshire Bull Terriers are no longer confined to the British Isles, and ownership now extends to Australia, Europe (especially Belgium, France, Germany and Holland), Scandinavia, New Zealand, to parts of the African continent and to many other countries. It is possibly in the United States of America, however, that there will be the greatest increase in the breed's popularity during the next decade or so.

Certain similarities exist between the position in the United Kingdom immediately after World War II, and the breed's present development in the United States of America, where it was recognised by the American Kennel Club in 1973. In the United Kingdom the breed developed from the Bull and Terrier used in organised dog fighting and variously known as 'The Fighting Terrier', 'The Stafford' and 'The Pit Dog'. Probably the names 'Pit Dog' or 'Pit Bull Terrier' were the most popular and widely used throughout the dog-fighting areas of England.

When the first fighting dogs of this type were taken to America by their owners, they formed the nucleus of dogs that became known as the American Pit Bull Terrier. According to some sources, the American Pit Bull Terrier was the result of crossing the original English Bull Dog with the Old English White Terrier, with, it is rumoured, the introduction of the Spanish Pointer! I doubt the veracity of such statements; in my view the dogs exported to America during the later part of the nineteenth century were essentially Bull and Terriers, which were, as has been previously described, an amalgam of the indigenous Bulldog and a wide variety of terrier-type animals. Certainly the early nineteenth-century Bulldog genes had contributed greatly to the physical, mental and temperamental characteristics of these dogs, but so had various types of British terrier. To be more specific than this would be pure conjecture.

It is probably true, however, that a number of owners of fighting dogs in the United Kingdom decided to emigrate to the United States of America in an effort to capitalise on the undoubted gladiatorial qualities of their Bull and Terriers. The best documented information concerns Cockney Charlie with his dog Pilot, but there were many others. By 1900 the dogs had become established as the American Pit Bull Terrier, and their popularity was continuing to increase. Impromptu dog fights, staged in tavern cellars and in secluded rural settings, developed into highly organised canine combats, despite the illegality of dog fighting in many American states.

By 1936 an American Pit Bull Terrier Standard appeared; exactly a year after the British Kennel Club had approved a Standard for the Staffordshire Bull Terrier. There is little similarity between the two Standards and the American version, which was not of course approved by the American Kennel Club, is given below.

American Pit Bull Terrier Standard
(Approved by the United Kennel Club, Inc, 1936)

Head   Medium length, brick-like in shape, skull flat and widest at the ears, with prominent cheeks, free from wrinkles.

Muzzle   Square, wide and deep, well pronounced jaws, displaying strength. Upper teeth to meet tightly over lower teeth, outside in front.

Ears   Cropped or uncropped (not important), should be set high on head, and free from .wrinkles.

Eyes   Dark and round; should be set far apart low down on skull.

Nose   Black preferred with wide open nostrils.

Neck   Muscular, slightly arched, tapering from shoulder to head, free from looseness of skin.

Shoulders   Strong and muscular with wide sloping shoulder blades.

Back   Short and strong, slightly sloping from withers to rump. Slightly arched at loins which should be slightly tucked.

Chest   Deep but not too broad, with wide sprung ribs.

Ribs   Close, well sprung, with deep back ribs.

Tail   Short in comparison to size, set low and tapering to a fine point, not carried over the back.

Legs   Large round boned, with straight upright pasterns reasonably strong. Feet to be of medium size. Gait should be light and springy. No rolling or pacing.

Thighs Long with muscles developed. Hocks down and straight.
Coat Glossy, short and stiff to the touch.
Color Any color or marking permissible.
Weight Not important. Females preferred from thirty to fifty pounds. Males from thirty-five to sixty pounds.

Perhaps the more pragmatic among us would draw attention to the fact that this Standard seemed specifically suited to a fighting dog. A 'brick-like' head has connotations of toughness, besides shape, and such points as colour and weight were not important apart from the obvious fact that owners seldom matched their dogs against heavier specimens; as in pugilism the 'weigh-in' was of extreme importance. Two sections are of great interest: those concerning the mouth and the thighs.

Evidently the dog-fighting fraternity, which was mainly responsible for this document, insisted on a strong level mouth with the top incisors meeting tightly over the bottom incisor teeth; it also required long thighs with well-developed muscles and hocks 'down and straight'. These are features of the Stafford anatomy which are just as important today. If we deviate from our present Standard in this respect we will do the breed a great disservice.

A comparison of this Standard with our own will show significant differences between the breeds in the United Kingdom and in America at that stage of their development. American Staffordshire Terriers developed along quite different lines from the British Staffordshire Bull Terriers, and it was not until 1973 that the Staffordshire Bull Terrier, mainly the result of importing dogs from the United Kingdom, was recognised by the American Kennel Club. The American Staffordshire Terrier is now of course quite a different breed; its original Standard is given below, with the permission of the AKC.

Description and Standard of Points
(Adopted by the Staffordshire Terrier Club of America and
Approved by the American Kennel Club, 10 June, 1936)

General impression The Staffordshire Terrier should give the impression of: great strength for his size; a well put-together dog, muscular, but agile and graceful, keenly alive to his surroundings. He should be stocky, not long-legged or racy in outline. His courage is proverbial.

Head   Medium length, deep through, broad skull, very pronounced check muscles, distinct stop; and ears are set high.

Ears   Cropped or uncropped, the latter preferred. Uncropped ears should be short and held half rose or prick. Full drop to be penalized.

Eyes   Dark and round, low down in skull and set far apart. No pink eyelids.

Muzzle   Medium length, rounded on upper side to fall away abruptly below eyes. Jaws well-defined. Under jaw to be strong and have biting power. Lips close and even, no looseness. Upper teeth to meet tightly outside lower teeth in front. Nose definitely black.

Neck   Heavy, slightly arched, tapering from shoulders to back of skull. No looseness of skin. Medium length.

Shoulders   Strong and muscular with blades wide and sloping.

Back   Fairly short. Slight sloping from withers to rump with gentle short slope at rump to base of tail. Loins slightly tucked.

Body   Well sprung ribs, deep in rear. All ribs close together. Forelegs set rather wide apart to permit of chest development. Chest deep and broad.

Tail   Short in comparison to size, low set, tapering to a fine point; not curled or held over back. Not docked.

Legs   The front legs should be straight, large or round bones, pastern upright. No resemblance of bend in front. Hind quarters well-muscled, let down at hocks, turning neither in nor out. Feet of moderate size, well-arched and compact. Gait must be springy but without roll or pace.

Coat   Short, close, stiff to the touch, and glossy.

Color   Any color, solid, parti, or patched is permissible, but all white, more than 80 per cent white, black-and-tan, and liver not to be encouraged.

Size   Height and weight should be in proportion. A height of about eighteen (18) to nineteen (19) inches at shoulders for the male and seventeen (17) to eighteen (18) inches for the female is to be considered preferable.

Faults   Faults to be penalized are Dudley nose, light or pink eyes, tail too long or badly carried, undershot or overshot mouths.

A major obstacle to the growth of Staffordshire Bull Terriers in the United States are the complications surrounding the existence of two 'ruling bodies', the Staffordshire Bull Terrier Club of America and the Staffordshire Bull Terrier Club of USA. These two bodies have only recently held out the olive branch to each other, and there is still a feeling that the doves perched on the shoulders of the opposing emissaries could quickly be transformed into Staffordshire Bull Terriers! However, I hope my assessment of the situation tends towards pessimism. On 14 October 1979 the first co-sponsored match between the two clubs took place in Sun Valley, California, with Miss Ellenor May Gesler as the judge; this event may have been the first step towards future co-operation between the two bodies. A second co-sponsored match was held, again in Sun Valley, on 20 January 1980, with Mrs Yvonne Reeder of Australia as judge, and a third co-sponsored match with a British judge has now taken place. The latest information suggests that there will soon be one parent club for the breed in the United States which will be known as The Staffordshire Bull Terrier Club Inc.

The tremendous size of the country and the distances to be travelled do not ameliorate the problems. Since the breed was accepted by the American Kennel Club, a number of English judges have officiated at American shows. Although, somewhat naturally, there is a wide divergence of opinion in their assessment of the American dogs compared with their British counterparts, there seems to be general agreement that the breed as a whole needs to progress considerably before it reaches British standards. There are, however, some excellent Staffords in the United States, and their numbers will undoubtedly increase.

Little emphasis appears to have been made by visiting judges on the small, but subtle, differences between the two breed Standards. The American Kennel Club Breed Standard is as follows:

The Staffordshire Bull Terrier Breed Standard in the United States of America

Characteristics From the past history of the Staffordshire Bull Terrier, the modern dog draws its character of indomitable courage, high intelligence, and tenacity. This, coupled with its affection for its friends, and children in particular, its off-duty quietness and trustworthy stability, makes it a foremost all-purpose dog.

General appearance The Staffordshire Bull Terrier is a smooth-coated dog. It should be of great strength for its size and, although muscular, should be active and agile.

Head and skull Short, deep through, broad skull, very pronounced cheek muscles, distinct stop, short foreface, black nose. Pink (Dudley) nose to be considered a serious fault.

Eyes Dark preferable, but may bear some relation to coat color. Round, of medium size, and set to look straight ahead. Light eyes or pink eye rims to be considered a fault, except that where the coat surrounding the eye is white the eye rim may be pink.

Ears Rose or half-pricked and not large. Full drop or full prick to be considered a serious fault.

Mouth A bite in which the outer side of the lower incisors touches the inner side of the upper incisors. The lips should be tight and clean. The badly undershot or overshot bite is a serious fault.

Neck Muscular, rather short, clean in outline and gradually widening toward the shoulders.

Forequarters Legs straight and well boned, set rather far apart, without looseness at the shoulders and showing no weakness at the pasterns, from which point the feet turn out a little.

Body The body is close coupled, with a level topline, wide front, deep brisket and well sprung ribs being rather light in the loins.

Hindquarters The hindquarters should be well muscled, hocks let down with stifles well bent. Legs should be parallel when viewed from behind.

Feet The feet should be well padded, strong and of medium size. Dewclaws, if any, on the hind legs are generally removed. Dewclaws on the forelegs may be removed.

Tail The tail is undocked, of medium length, low set, tapering to a point and carried rather low. It should not curl much and may be likened to an old-fashioned pump handle. A tail that is too long or badly curled is a fault.

Coat Smooth, short and close to the skin, not to be trimmed or de-whiskered.

Color Red, fawn, white, black or blue, or any of these colors with white. Any shade of brindle or any shade of brindle with white. Black-and-tan or liver color to be disqualified.

Size Weight: Dogs, 28 to 38 pounds; bitches, 24 to 34 pounds. Height at shoulder: 14 to 16 inches, these heights being related to weights. Non-conformity with these limits is a fault.

Disqualifications Black-and-tan or liver color.

On cursory examination this Standard appears similar to our own, but there are minor differences, detailed overleaf.

Mouth
Although the wording is slightly different in the two Standards it means approximately the same, except that in the American Standard the badly undershot or overshot bite is considered 'a serious fault', whereas in the British Standard dogs that are badly undershot or badly overshot, as defined in the Standard, are debarred from winning any prize whatsoever.

Nose
The pink (Dudley) nose is considered to be a serious fault in the American Standard whereas in the British Standard it debars a dog from winning any prize whatsoever.

Eyes
Both Standards stipulate that light eyes or pink eye rims are to be considered faults, but the American Standard adds 'except that where the coat surrounding the eye is white the eye rim may be pink'.

Colour
While the British Standard states that black-and-tan or liver colour should not be encouraged, the American Standard specifically states that dogs with this coat colour should be disqualified.

Finally, there is no mention in the American Standard of the note contained in all British Standards that 'male animals should have two apparently normal testicles fully descended into the scrotum'.

It may well be that some of the changes made to the British Standard by the Americans, who had the advantage of formulating their Standard some twenty-five years later, may be considered advantageous. In this country I think there would certainly be some arguments about the complete disqualification of dogs which are black-and-tan or liver colour; there are differing views on this subject and controversy also surrounds what actually constitutes a real Dudley nose.

During the past few years there appears in Britain to have been a high percentage of bad mouths, possibly because of the advice of a few professed experts who advise breeders to use undershot stud dogs. If the amendment to the British Standard was to exacerbate this problem, then I feel sure that many breeders and exhibitors in this country would deplore it.

One of the great differences between the breed in the two countries is the method of achieving the status of champion. In Britain it is necessary for a Stafford to win three challenge certificates under different judges to achieve this status, and it may be pertinent to state that during 1976 only eleven dogs became champions, in 1977 there were fifteen, in 1978 there were eight, in 1979 eleven and in 1980 eleven. These figures must be considered in the light of over two thousand new registrations in the breed each year, a figure that will probably increase towards the end of the present decade.

Challenge certificates are awarded to the best dog in the breed and the best bitch in the breed at championship shows, which may be organised, subject to Kennel Club approval, by either the general championship show committees or any of the fifteen specialist breed clubs operating throughout the United Kingdom. The number of challenge certificates awarded to each breed is determined by the Kennel Club and depends largely on the number of Ch show breed entries. In 1979, for example, challenge certificates for Staffords were on offer at twenty-five general championship shows and six specialist championship shows, while in 1981, approval has been given for challenge certificates to be awarded at twenty-six general championship shows and seven championship shows organised by specialist breed clubs. Any judge awarding challenge certificates must be approved by the Kennel Club and normally would only award certificates once every nine months in respect of an individual breed. Each of the fifteen specialist breed clubs annually draws up a list of judges who are placed in different categories, with one for those judges who, in the club's view, are capable of awarding challenge certificates to the breed.

The majority of such judges are 'specialist' judges who, in the main, judge Staffordshire Bull Terriers and no other breeds; the number of 'all-rounders', those prepared to judge most breeds (loosely the equivalent of the American Kennel Club Group judge), are not popular in the breed for a number of reasons. There are, of course, a few all-rounders who are quite knowledgeable about Staffords, and conversely there are a number of specialists who may not be considered to be ideally suited to award challenge certificates.

In the United States the situation is quite different. A dog becomes a champion by gaining a total of fifteen points, which includes two majors. The number of points awarded depends on the type of show and on the number of dogs entered. Another great difference is that US judges for their 'Pointers', which are roughly the equivalent of our championship shows, are seldom Staffordshire Bull Terrier specialists. In order to judge Staffords at American championship shows, a judge needs to be conversant with terrier breeds generally, and this can mean that such judges are not necessarily acquainted with detailed breed type. Although the Staffordshire Bull Terrier is included in the terrier group it is, as its name suggests, an amalgam of the Bulldog and the terrier and therefore does not fall easily into the terrier grouping, although it is nearer this group than any other.

I do not wish to enter into a discussion on the virtues of the specialist *vis-à-vis* the all-rounder, as most experienced fanciers are well aware of all the arguments. For the sake of the beginner in the breed, it should be stated that the specialist is generally a breeder and exhibitor, who, because of his closer association with a particular breed, must inevitably know more of 'breed type' than one who is dealing with a wide variety of breeds. It is, of course, argued that the specialist judge may become so obsessed with breed type that he fails to recognise shortcomings in general soundness, while the all-rounder, not so conversant with breed type, may concentrate on general soundness. The truth is that it is impossible to generalise; the best specialists are normally better informed about their breed but may be at a disadvantage as they only judge on a few occasions each year, whereas the all-rounder may be officiating each week, thus gaining valuable experience of the techniques of judging and of general canine anatomy.

Statuette of a fighting dog by Valton, about 1850

Georgia, daughter of Tiara of Roxette, at ten months (*Panther Photographic International*)

Staffords make good family pets

Ch Skean Dhu, owned by Mr G. Carter and bred by Mrs P. B. Grotrain in
1978. This striking black dog was the top Stafford of 1980

(*above*) Ch Red Rum, owned by Mr and Mrs T. Ruddie and bred by David Birchall. Gained his title at Crufts 1980 and sired Ch Goldwyn Leading Star; (*right*) Ch Goldwyn Leading Star, owned and bred by Mr and Mrs P. Wall in 1978, the seventh generation of bitches produced by these breeders. Already awarded seven challenge certificates and Best of Breed at Crufts 1981

In the United Kingdom almost all Staffords are exhibited by their owners or by one of their associates; in the United States the professional handler is used more often. The familiar broad, studded collar, a tradition of the British Staffordshire Bull Terrier, is not generally used in American rings, where a short thin leash is preferred.

The American Kennel Club, accommodated at 51 Madison Avenue, New York, NY 10010, was founded in September 1884 as a non-profit making organisation whose main objective was to adopt and enforce rules and regulations governing dog shows, obedience trials and field trials. The AKC keeps the official register of pure bred dogs in the United States and is responsible for approving judges for recognised dog shows. It publishes two monthly magazines, the *AKC Gazette*, which contains a record of championship points earned, and the Stud Book Register. The *AKC Gazette* covers a wider spectrum of activity than its British counterpart as it includes, in addition to the official information, breed columns written by international breed clubs and show and obedience columns, which discuss the topical problems of the day, together with feature articles which may be of interest to breeders and exhibitors.

Also of interest to Stafford enthusiasts are the tri-annual magazine published by the SBTCA, *Staff Status*, and the Bulletin of the SBTC/USA appearing quarterly. These magazines, which often include contributions from Britain, are widely read by owners of Staffordshire Bull Terriers both in the United States and elsewhere. They are profusely illustrated with photographs of contemporary dogs.

As I conclude this chapter I have received confirmation that the Staffordshire Bull Terrier Club Inc has been officially launched, combining the previous two breed clubs. The two magazines have also been incorporated into a new publication co-edited by Judi Daniels and Irma Rosenfield – *United We Stand*.

12

THE FUTURE OF THE BREED

The growth in interest in Staffordshire Bull Terriers appears to have accelerated during the past two years, as is apparent from the increased membership of breed clubs, the larger show entries and urgent requests for stock and relevant reading material.

Breed registrations have already climbed into third place in the Kennel Club's 'Terrier League Table' behind West Highland White Terriers and Cairn Terriers, and it is possible that by the end of the decade Staffords will be the foremost terrier breed. In 1980 and 1981 the Stafford entries for Crufts exceeded those of any other terrier breed, and the trend is continuing at most championship shows. It may seem somewhat reckless to make such a forecast but the trends over the past two decades suggest that the breed could achieve popularity greater than the most optimistic forecasts of those stalwarts who met in Cradley Heath in 1935 to form the first breed club.

Although this increasing popularity may not surprise experienced Stafford enthusiasts who are well aware of the qualities of their dogs, this knowledge seems to have spread more generally, and more and more people are now attracted to the breed. Its short coat, which makes it comparatively easy to care for; its size, which is convenient for the modern home; its adaptability to any form or change of environment; the ease with which it can be trained and its undoubted safety with, and tolerance of, children, combined with many less tangible qualities, add up to make the Staffordshire Bull Terrier a strong candidate for the title of the best all-round breed available.

There are, of course, dangers in this situation. Consider what has happened to other breeds that have gained relatively quick popularity. Many of the dogs of such breeds are pale imitations of their ancestors; a few are absolute travesties. One of the ancestors of the Stafford, the magnificent bulldog of the early nineteenth century, bears little resemblance to today's breed of the same name, which is now included in the Kennel Club's utility group of non-sporting breeds.

Perhaps the real danger is that, either by indiscriminate breeding or by misdirected selective breeding, some of those physical and mental characteristics which make the Stafford such an attractive dog, may disappear. Despite changes over the past forty years, the Staffordshire Bull Terrier appears to have retained two fundamental characteristics: his 'naturalism' and his 'humanism'. Although difficult to analyse, these are the breed's most important virtues. There are certainly more handsome dogs than the Staffordshire Bull Terrier, but I think that the best specimens of the breed possess classical outlines and if some of the photographs reproduced in this book are studied even the cynics may accept that this is so.

There have, of course, been changes which many enthusiasts consider to be retrograde. The best dogs of the 1930s, and to a lesser extent of the 1940s, were taller at the shoulder than most modern dogs, they were more terrier-like, they had a smaller girth of skull and possessed greater agility than some of our modern dogs. It will be remembered that until 1949 the original Standard, conceived in 1935, was still in being and allowed much wider margins in the heights and weights of the dogs. The 1949 Standard, with its specific relationship between size and weight, certainly produced greater uniformity; it has also produced some dogs which many consider to be too small and heavy, lacking the essential relationship of terrier and bulldog and the required strength and agility.

Undoubtedly one of the most serious threats to the future of the breed is the problem surrounding the Height/Weight clause in the present Standard. Although this has been dealt with in Chapter 3, its importance cannot be over-emphasised. For many years now the majority of winning dogs diverge widely from the specifications of the clause that states: 'Weight: dogs 12.7–17.24k (28–38lb); bitches 10.59–15.42k (24–34lb). Height (at shoulder): 35.56–40.64cm (14–16in) *these heights being related to the weights.*' (The italics are mine!)

It is surprising that even today some owners believe that their dogs comply with this clause if, for example, they measure 35.5cm (14in) at the shoulder and weigh 17.2k (38lb) or, in the case of bitches, are 35.5cm (14in) at the shoulder and weigh 15.4k (34lb). If this were so it would be equally acceptable to have a 40.6cm (16in) dog weighing 12.7k (28lb) and a 40.6cm (16in) bitch weighing only 10.9k (24lb)! These are, of course, the extremes and discount the important fact that the heights should be related to the weights.

The 35.6cm (14in) dog should weigh only 12.7k (28lb), and the 35.6cm (14in) bitch, 10.9k (24lb); only the 40.6cm (16in) dog and the 40.6cm (16in) bitch should scale the top weights allowable in the Standard of 17.2k (38lb) and 15.4k (34lb) respectively. If a 35.6cm (14in) dog weighing 17.2k (38lb) is compared with a 40.6cm (16in) dog weighing 12.7k (28lb), completely different animals would be revealed and standardisation would be impossible.

In practice, judges have interpreted this clause of the Standard somewhat flexibly. Almost all dogs winning today are heavier than the related weight acceptable for their height; some really fit dogs carrying hardly any excess fat, may be only a few pounds above the weight limit, but others can be up to 10lb overweight. This may not appear a tremendous amount, but even at the upper limit it would represent 26 per cent overweight and at the lower limit as much as 41 per cent! Unfortunately, experience has shown that attempts to rationalise the situation have been abortive and have often generated so much friction that they have been counterproductive. Nevertheless, the situation is such that it must attract some urgent debate if the Breed Standard is to remain a serious document.

The problem is that some breeders have produced winning specimens so much smaller and heavier than originally intended that they would need completely to re-think their breeding programmes if their stock were to comply with this clause of the Standard. At the other end of the scale remain a few old-timers who are fully convinced that the lighter, terrier-type dog, not now so popular in the show-ring, is nearer the real fighting Stafford of yesteryear.

Some fanciers quote the measurements of Jim the Dandy,

which, at two and a half years old, stood 44.45cm (17½in) high at the shoulder, weighed about 14.97k (33lb) and had only a girth of skull of 43.18cm (17in), a measurement that would be considered derisory on a present-day dog of lesser height. Although opinions differ whether Jim the Dandy was the blueprint for the 1935 Standard, it seems true that this dog influenced the content of the original Standard even if not all would agree with the view of his owner, the late Jack Barnard, that he was 'the most perfect specimen of the day'.

There are those who feel that if the trend of the past forty-five years is to continue, we may in another forty-five years produce smaller and heavier Staffordshire Bull Terriers that lack the essential strength and agility which are probably the most significant physical attributes of the breed.

Perhaps a good old English compromise is necessary for a good old English breed. My own view is that there should be a *desired* height of 40.6cm (16in) and no specific weight limits, but a proviso that all dogs should be well balanced. Unfortunately any written term is liable to different interpretation, and the word 'balanced' certainly comes into this category, but an amendment to the Height/Weight clause on the following lines might prove acceptable:

The desired height (at the withers) should be 40.6cm (16in) (dogs) and 39.4cm (15½in) bitches with slight variations being acceptable. There is no weight limit but there should be an impression of great substance and balance commensurate with size. Dogs should appear masculine and bitches feminine.

Such an alteration would still allow for a degree of flexibility but would eventually produce a greater degree of standardisation. Obviously the 36.8cm (14½in) bitch weighing 17.2k (38lb) would be placed at a disadvantage, but conversely the 42cm (16½in) dog weighing 20.4k (45lb) would be more acceptable than at present. I also take the view that, as is the practice in certain other Standards, dogs should appear masculine and bitches feminine. Even in a fighting breed I feel that there should be a distinction between the physical appearance of sexes; even our Sex Discrimination Act doesn't preclude this! There has, during past years, been a tendency on the part of certain breeders to produce bitches with as great a girth of skull as possible, and in my view this is a retrograde step if it affects balance and femininity.

As a representative on the Staffordshire Bull Terrier Breed Council of Great Britain and Northern Ireland, I am not optimistic about the possibility of achieving unanimity in such a proposal; owners of Staffords, rather like their dogs, possess a tremendous degree of tenacity; if they have a strongly held view they find it difficult to compromise! I would not have it any other way.

Paradoxically, the anatomical problems of the breed are those of thirty years ago, and it is of some concern that the two principal faults associated with the breed, those of undershot mouths and straight stifles, still appear. Writers of thirty years ago were referring to these two major faults and, although there may have been periods of improvement, such faults still exist and will continue to exist as long as breeders fail to be selective enough in their operations. The only certain way of eliminating undershot mouths is to refuse to breed from undershot stock, and those who advocate otherwise are doing a disservice to the breed.

Authoritative writers of the 1940s seem to agree that Staffordshires at that time had in general a rear action which was inferior to that of many other varieties of terrier. The position certainly improved, and some of our best dogs had excellent front and rear actions. I have, however, noticed at recent championship shows that there are a good number of dogs which are either straight stifled or cow hocked, and again this is a tendency to be avoided in the future.

One of the more optimistic signs for the future is that, although there are many rugged individualists within the breed and many different viewpoints on certain aspects of it, overriding all these differences is a camaraderie manifested by the desire of most breeders and exhibitors to help their fellows in any way possible. The breed is not yet bedevilled, and I hope it never will be, with the large breeders; the small kennel and the individual owner are the general rule. We must guard against the dealers entering the scene, and certainly our breed clubs should be giving as much publicity as possible to the necessity of purchasing stock from bona fide breeders. There is a danger that, when under pressure of demand for puppies exceeding the supply, breeders may produce litters for commercial gain, and intending purchasers should resolve only to buy from established breeders who are jealous of their reputations. Nevertheless this is possibly a temporary stage and no doubt the situation will resolve itself before long.

THE PRESENT POSITION

The number of Staffordshires kept continues to grow, a sure sign of satisfaction from all who are dog lovers. Moreover, it has not been spoilt by showing. Agreed, there are still the heavily built dogs, which often grow too fat for active running or walking. At the other extreme, there are the light weight dogs, which follow the terrier style and which keep on being very active to a ripe old age.

The choice is left to the owner and breeder, but the strong head and well developed body are certainly the requirements today. Overall fitness and the correct temperament are also essential breed characteristics.

APPENDICES

4 MATING & WHELPING CHART

	1	2	3	4	5	6	7	8	9	10	11	12	13	14	15	16	17	18	19	20	21	22	23	24	25	26	27	28	29	30	31
Mated Jan.	1	2	3	4	5	6	7	8	9	10	11	12	13	14	15	16	17	18	19	20	21	22	23	24	25	26	27	28	29	30	31
Litter due Mar.	5	6	7	8	9	10	11	12	13	14	15	16	17	18	19	20	21	22	23	24	25	26	27	28	29	30	31	Apr. 1	2	3	4
Mated Feb.	1	2	3	4	5	6	7	8	9	10	11	12	13	14	15	16	17	18	19	20	21	22	23	24	25	26	27	28			
Litter due Apr.	5	6	7	8	9	10	11	12	13	14	15	16	17	18	19	20	21	22	23	24	25	26	27	28	29	30	May 1	2			
Mated Mar.	1	2	3	4	5	6	7	8	9	10	11	12	13	14	15	16	17	18	19	20	21	22	23	24	25	26	27	28	29	30	31
Litter due May	3	4	5	6	7	8	9	10	11	12	13	14	15	16	17	18	19	20	21	22	23	24	25	26	27	28	29	30	31	June 1	2
Mated Apr.	1	2	3	4	5	6	7	8	9	10	11	12	13	14	15	16	17	18	19	20	21	22	23	24	25	26	27	28	29	30	
Litter due June	3	4	5	6	7	8	9	10	11	12	13	14	15	16	17	18	19	20	21	22	23	24	25	26	27	28	29	30	July 1	2	
Mated May	1	2	3	4	5	6	7	8	9	10	11	12	13	14	15	16	17	18	19	20	21	22	23	24	25	26	27	28	29	30	31
Litter due July	3	4	5	6	7	8	9	10	11	12	13	14	15	16	17	18	19	20	21	22	23	24	25	26	27	28	29	30	31	Aug. 1	2
Mated June	1	2	3	4	5	6	7	8	9	10	11	12	13	14	15	16	17	18	19	20	21	22	23	24	25	26	27	28	29	30	
Litter due Aug.	3	4	5	6	7	8	9	10	11	12	13	14	15	16	17	18	19	20	21	22	23	24	25	26	27	28	29	30	31	Sept. 1	
Mated July	1	2	3	4	5	6	7	8	9	10	11	12	13	14	15	16	17	18	19	20	21	22	23	24	25	26	27	28	29	30	31
Litter due Sept.	2	3	4	5	6	7	8	9	10	11	12	13	14	15	16	17	18	19	20	21	22	23	24	25	26	27	28	29	30	Oct. 1	2
Mated Aug.	1	2	3	4	5	6	7	8	9	10	11	12	13	14	15	16	17	18	19	20	21	22	23	24	25	26	27	28	29	30	31
Litter due Oct.	3	4	5	6	7	8	9	10	11	12	13	14	15	16	17	18	19	20	21	22	23	24	25	26	27	28	29	30	31	Nov. 1	2
Mated Sept.	1	2	3	4	5	6	7	8	9	10	11	12	13	14	15	16	17	18	19	20	21	22	23	24	25	26	27	28	29	30	
Litter due Nov.	3	4	5	6	7	8	9	10	11	12	13	14	15	16	17	18	19	20	21	22	23	24	25	26	27	28	29	30	Dec. 1	2	
Mated Oct.	1	2	3	4	5	6	7	8	9	10	11	12	13	14	15	16	17	18	19	20	21	22	23	24	25	26	27	28	29	30	31
Mated Dec.	3	4	5	6	7	8	9	10	11	12	13	14	15	16	17	18	19	20	21	22	23	24	25	26	27	28	29	30	31	Jan. 1	2
Mated Nov.	1	2	3	4	5	6	7	8	9	10	11	12	13	14	15	16	17	18	19	20	21	22	23	24	25	26	27	28	29	30	
Litter due Jan.	3	4	5	6	7	8	9	10	11	12	13	14	15	16	17	18	19	20	21	22	23	24	25	26	27	28	29	30	31	Feb. 1	
Mated Dec.	1	2	3	4	5	6	7	8	9	10	11	12	13	14	15	16	17	18	19	20	21	22	23	24	25	26	27	28	29	30	31
Litter due Feb.	2	3	4	5	6	7	8	9	10	11	12	13	14	15	16	17	18	19	20	21	22	23	24	25	26	27	28	Mar. 1	2	3	4

5 REGULATIONS FOR THE DEFINITIONS OF CLASSES

Championship and Other Open Shows

Wins in variety classes do not count for entry in breed classes, but when entering for variety classes, wins in both breed and variety classes must be counted. A variety class is one in which more than one breed can complete. A first prize does not include a special prize of whatever value.

In estimating the number of prizes won, all wins up to seven days before the date of closing of entries shall be counted when entering for any class. Wins at championship shows in breed classes where challenge certificates are not on offer shall be counted as wins at open shows.

Note *In the following definitions, a challenge certificate includes any show award that counts towards the title of Champion under the rules of any governing body recognised by the Kennel Club.*

With these provisos the following are the definitions of certain classes:

Minor Puppy For dogs of six and not exceeding nine calendar months of age on the first day of the show.

Puppy For dogs of six and not exceeding twelve calendar months of age on the first day of the show.

Junior For dogs of six and not exceeding eighteen calendar months of age on the first day of the show.

Maiden For dogs which have not won a challenge certificate or a first prize at an open or championship show. (Puppy, Special Puppy, Minor Puppy and Special Minor Puppy classes excepted.)

Novice For dogs which have not won a challenge certificate or three or more first prizes at an open or championship show. (Puppy, Special Puppy, Minor Puppy and Special Minor Puppy classes excepted.)

Tyro For dogs which have not won a challenge certificate or five or more first prizes at open shows. (Puppy, Special Puppy, Minor Puppy and Special Minor Puppy classes excepted.)

Debutant For dogs which have not won a challenge certificate or a first prize at a championship show. (Puppy, Special Puppy, Minor Puppy and Special Minor Puppy classes excepted.)

Undergraduate For dogs which have not won a challenge certificate or three or more first prizes at championship shows. (Puppy, Special Puppy, Minor Puppy and Special Minor Puppy classes excepted.)

Graduate For dogs which have not won a challenge certificate or four or more first prizes at championship shows in Graduate, Post-graduate, Minor Limit, Mid-limit, Limit and Open classes, whether restricted or not.

Post-graduate For dogs which have not won a challenge certificate or five or more first prizes at championship shows in Post-graduate, Minor Limit, Mid-limit, Limit and Open classes, whether restricted or not.

Minor Limit For dogs which have not won two challenge certificates or three or more first prizes in all at championship shows in Minor Limit, Mid-limit, Limit and Open classes, confined to the breed, whether restricted or not, at shows where challenge certificates were offered for the breed.

Mid-limit For dogs which have not won three challenge certificates or five or more first prizes in all at championship shows in Mid-limit, Limit and Open classes, confined to the breed, whether restricted or not, at shows where challenge certificates were offered for the breed.

Limit For dogs which have not won three challenge certificates under three different judges or seven or more first prizes in all, at championship shows in Limit and Open classes, confined to the breed, whether restricted or not, at shows where challenge certificates were offered for the breed.

Open For all dogs of the breeds for which the class is provided and eligible for entry at the show.

Veteran For dogs of an age specified in the schedule but not less than five years on the first day of the show.

Field Trial For dogs which have won prizes, awards of honour, diplomas of merit, or certificates of merit in actual competition at a field trial held under Kennel Club or Irish Kennel Club Field Trial Rules and Regulations.

Brace For two exhibits (either sex or mixed) of one breed belonging to the same exhibitor, each exhibit having been entered in some class other than Brace or Team.

Team For three or more exhibits (either sex or mixed) of one breed belonging to the same exhibitor, each exhibit having been entered in some class other than Brace or Team.

Sweepstake For Brace, Team, Stud Dog, Brood Bitch, Veteran and Breeders classes only, in which the entry fees may be given as prize money in such proportion as the show committee may determine.

Subject to the above and to any regulations, show committees may offer such prizes and make such classification and definitions thereof as they think fit, except that:

1 All classes advertised in the schedule of the show must be clearly defined in the schedule, in accordance with the Kennel Club Show Regulations.

2 If any class be provided with a definition other than those defined above, the word 'Special' must precede the name of such class.

3 The words 'Grand', 'Champion' or 'Challenge' must not be used in the designation of any class or prize for which an entrance fee is charged and for which entry has to be made prior to the day of the show.

4 No Field Trial class other than that defined above shall be permitted.

Limited and Sanction Shows

Wins in variety classes do not count for entry in breed classes, but when entering for variety classes, wins in both breed and variety classes must be counted. A variety class is one in which more than one breed can compete. A first prize does not include a special prize of whatever value.

In estimating the number of prizes won, all wins up to seven days before the date of closing of entries shall be counted when entering for any class.

Note *No class higher than Post-graduate may be offered at a sanction show. Minor Limit, Mid-limit, Limit and Open classes must not be offered at sanction shows. No dog is eligible for exhibition at a limited or sanction show which has won a challenge certificate or obtained any show award that counts towards the title of Champion under the rules of any governing body recognised by the Kennel Club.*

With these provisos the following are the definitions of certain classes:

Minor Puppy For dogs of six and not exceeding nine calendar months of age on the first day of the show.

Puppy For dogs of six and not exceeding twelve calendar months of age on the first day of the show.

Junior For dogs of six and not exceeding eighteen calendar months of age on the first day of the show.

Maiden For dogs which have not won a first prize at any show. (Puppy, Special Puppy, Minor Puppy and Special Minor Puppy classes excepted.)

Novice For dogs which have not won three or more first prizes at any show or shows. (Puppy, Special Puppy, Minor Puppy and Special Minor Puppy classes excepted.)

Tyro For dogs which have not won five or more first prizes at any show or shows. (Puppy, Special Puppy, Minor Puppy and Special Minor Puppy classes excepted.)

Debutant For dogs which have not won a first prize at an open or championship show. (Puppy, Special Puppy, Minor Puppy and Special Minor Puppy classes excepted.)

Undergraduate For dogs which have not won three or more first prizes at open or championship shows. (Puppy, Special Puppy, Minor Puppy and Special Minor Puppy classes excepted.)

Graduate For dogs which have not won four or more first prizes at open or championship shows in Graduate, Post-graduate, Minor Limit, Mid-limit, Limit and Open classes, whether restricted or not.

Post-graduate For dogs which have not won five or more first prizes at open and championship shows in Post-graduate, Graduate, Minor Limit, Mid-limit, Limit and Open classes, whether restricted or not.

Minor Limit For dogs which have not won three or more first prizes at open or championship shows in Minor Limit, Mid-limit, Limit and Open classes, confined to the breed, whether restricted or not.

Mid-limit For dogs which have not won five or more first prizes in all at open and championship shows in Mid-limit, Limit and Open classes, confined to the breed, whether restricted or not.

Limit For dogs which have not won seven or more first prizes in all at open and championship shows in Limit and Open classes, confined to the breed, whether restricted or not.

Open For all dogs of the breeds for which the class is provided and eligible for entry at the show.

Veteran For dogs of any age specified in the schedule but not less than five years on the first day of the show.

Field Trial For dogs which have won prizes, awards of honour, diplomas of merit or certificates of merit, in actual competition at a field trial held under Kennel Club or Irish Kennel Club Field Trial Rules and Regulations.

Brace For two exhibits (either sex or mixed) of one breed belonging to the same exhibitor, each exhibit having been entered in some class other than Brace or Team.

Team For three or more exhibits (either sex or mixed) of one breed belonging to the same exhibitor, each exhibit having been entered in some class other than Brace or Team.

Sweepstake For Brace, Team, Stud Dog, Brood Bitch, Veteran and Breeders classes only, in which the entry fees are given as the prize money in such proportion as the show committee may determine.

Subject to the above, and to any regulations, show committees may offer such prizes and make such classification and definitions thereof as they think fit, except that:

1 All classes advertised in the schedule of a show must be clearly defined in the schedule, in accordance with the Kennel Club Show Regulations.

2 If any class be provided with a definition other than those defined above, the word 'Special' must precede the name of such class.

3 The words 'Grand', 'Champion' or 'Challenge' must not be used in the designation of any class or prize for which an entrance fee is charged and for which entry has to be made prior to the day of the show.

4 No Field Trial class other than that defined above shall be permitted.

Extract from Kennel Club Regulations for Primary Shows

The following Regulations shall apply to all primary shows:

1 These shows must not commence earlier than 5 p.m., except on Saturdays and Sundays when they may commence at 2 p.m. and must conclude the same day. The dogs need not be benched.

2 There shall not be fewer than three awards and reserve on offer in every class. Printed awards may be given as prizes, must be white and overprinted 'Primary Show'.

3 The fee for holding each primary show is £2.50 (plus VAT).

4 Only bona fide members of the association, club or society holding the show may compete.

5 The show must not comprise more than eight classes. The highest which may be scheduled is Maiden.

6 Dogs which have won a first prize at any show (Puppy, Special Puppy, Minor Puppy and Special Minor Puppy classes excepted), challenge certificate or reserve challenge certificate may not compete at primary shows.

7 All dogs exhibited at these shows must be registered at the Kennel Club in accordance with Rule 5 of the Kennel Club Rules, and must be the property of the persons entering them. All entries must be correctly and properly made in accordance with the registration of the particular dogs, and the exhibitors must sign the declaration on the entry form.

8 In cases of change of ownership of a registered dog, the transfer to the exhibitor of such dog must be registered at the Kennel Club, and no such dogs will be eligible for exhibition at any primary show until such transfer has been registered.

9 A separate official entry form which must be an exact copy of the wording of the specimen entry form issued by the Kennel Club must be completed by every person(s) entering a dog(s) for competition.

10 Entries may be taken on the day of the show and a dog(s) must be eligible for the show at the time of entry for exhibition.

11 A catalogue of entries need not be produced. A record of the prizes and awards given with the completed entry forms for the show must be retained by the show secretary for at least twelve months from the day of the show.

6 EXTRACT FROM THE PROTECTION OF ANIMALS ACT 1911

An Act to consolidate, amend, and extend certain enactments relating to Animals and to Knackers; and to make further provision with respect thereto.

Be it enacted by the King's most Excellent Majesty, by and with the advice and consent of the Lords Spiritual and Temporal, and Commons, in this present Parliament assembled and by the authority of the same, as follows:

1 (1) If any person –

(a) shall cruelly beat, kick, ill-treat, over-ride, over-drive, over-load, torture, infuriate, or terrify any animal, or shall cause or procure, or, being the owner, permit any animal to be so used, or shall, by wantonly or unreasonably doing or omitting to do any act, or causing or procuring the commission of any act, cause any unnecessary suffering to be so caused to any animal; or

(b) shall convey or carry, or cause or procure, or, being the owner, permit to be conveyed or carried, any animal in such manner or position as to cause that animal any unnecessary suffering; or

(c) shall cause, procure, or assist at the fighting or baiting of any animal; or shall keep, use, manage, or act or assist in the management of, any premises or place for the purpose, or partly for the purpose of fighting or baiting any animal, or shall permit any premises or place to be so kept, managed, or used, or shall receive, or cause or procure any person to receive money for the admission of any person to such premises or place; or

(d) shall wilfully, without any reasonable cause or excuse, administer, or cause or procure, or being the owner permit, such administration of, any poisonous or injurious drug or substance to any animal, or shall wilfully, without any reasonable cause or excuse, cause any such substance to be taken by any animal; or

(e) shall subject, or cause or procure, or being the owner permit, to be subjected by any animal to any operation which is performed without due care and humanity;

such person shall be guilty of an offence of cruelty within the meaning of this Act, and shall be liable upon summary conviction to a fine not exceeding twenty-five pounds, or alternatively or in addition thereto, to be imprisoned, with or without hard labour, for any term not exceeding six months.

(2) For the purposes of this section, an owner shall be deemed to have permitted cruelty within the meaning of this Act if he shall have failed to exercise reasonable care and supervision in respect of the protection of the animal therefrom.

Provided that, where an owner is convicted of permitting cruelty within the meaning of this Act by reason only of his having failed to exercise such care and supervision, he shall not be liable to imprisonment without the option of a fine.

(3) Nothing in this section shall render illegal any act lawfully done under the Cruelty to Animals Act 1876, or shall apply –

(a) to the commission or omission of any act in the course of the destruction, or the preparation for destruction, of any animal as food for mankind, unless such destruction or such preparation was accompanied by the infliction of unnecessary suffering; or

(b) to the coursing or hunting of any captive animal, unless such animal is liberated in an injured, mutilated, or exhausted condition; but a captive animal shall not, for the purposes of this section, be deemed to be coursed or hunted before it is liberated for the purpose of being coursed or hunted, or after it has been re-captured, or if it is under control.

2 Where the owner of an animal is convicted of an offence of cruelty within the meaning of this Act, it shall be lawful for the court, if the court is satisfied that it would be cruel to keep the animal alive, to direct that the animal be destroyed, and to assign the animal to any suitable person for that purpose; and the person to whom such animal is so assigned shall, as soon as possible, destroy such animal, or cause or procure such animal to be destroyed, in his presence without unnecessary suffering. Any reasonable expenses incurred in destroying the animal may be ordered by the court to be paid by the owner, and thereupon shall be recoverable summarily as a civil debt;

Provided that, unless the owner assent, no order shall be made under this section except upon the evidence of a duly registered veterinary surgeon.

7 STAFFORDSHIRE BULL TERRIER CHAMPIONS 1939–1980

Year	Name	Sex	Sire	Dam	Owner	Breeder	Date of Birth
1939	Ch Game Laddie	D	Game Lad	Mad Molly	W. A. Boylan	W. A. Boylan	2.01.36
	Ch Gentleman Jim	D	Brindle Mick	Triton Judy	J. Mallen	Jack Dunn	27.05.37
	Ch Lady Eve	B	Barney	Gipsy	Joseph Dunn	J. Evans	10.06.35
	Ch Madcap Mischief	B	Ch Game Laddie	Timyke Mustard	Miss A. Harrison	W. A. Boylan	8.07.37
	Ch Midnight Gift	D	Game Bill	Blue Bell Bess	Mrs M. Beare	G. Ashman	22.07.37
1947	Ch Head Lad of Villmar	D	Vindictive Monty of Wyncroft	Fred's Fancy	R. Servat	Mr & Mrs J. Martin	2.03.45
	Ch Widneyland Kim	D	Ch Gentleman Jim	Game Judy	G. A. Dudley	H. Harris	8.03.44
	Ch Widneyland Model	B	Togo	White Bess	Mrs D. M. Payton-Smith	W. R. Marsh	4.01.44
1948	Ch Wychbury Red Cap	B	Ch Brigands Bo'sun	Rita's Pride	G. A. Dudley	J. Bloomer	20.09.46
	Ch Fearless Red of Bandits	D	Ch Gentleman Jim	Dee's Pegg	Mrs J. F. Gordon	H. Priest	22.07.44
	Ch Perfect Lady	B	Furnace Jake	Plucky Queen	A. Tryhorn	T. W. Cooper	14.03.44
	Ch Sandra's Boy	D	Bomber Command	Crossguns Sandra	C. Blackwell	C. Blackwell	10.11.44
	Ch Widneyland Ritver Ringleader	B	Ch Brigands Bo'sun	Uta of Roxana	A. P. Smith	Miss R. Vernon	17.06.46
1949	Ch Wychbury Kimbo	D	Ch Widneyland Kim	Wychbury Peggy	G. A. Dudley	G. A. Dudley	19.07.46
	Ch Wychbury Oak Beauty	B	Prince St John	Vindictive Flirt	G. A. Dudley	J. Birch	25.10.44
	Ch Brigands Bo'sun	D	Brindle Bill	Fredancer	A. P. Smith	J. Hall	14.06.43
	Ch Brigands Red Rogerson	D	Jolly Roger	Lady Juror	Mrs J. F Gordon	A. Brazenhill	1.09.45
	Ch Brindle Crescendo of Wychbury	D	Walters Gift	Brins Beast	G. A. Dudley	Mr & Mrs. W. Attwood	14.08.47
	Ch Brindle Mac	D	Boy Dan	Our Cissy	H. Ashton	N. Lever	10.01.45
	Ch Brinstock Sandy Bridget	B	Ch Game Laddie	Brinstock Bridget	W. A. Boylan	W. A. Boylan	23.04.47
	Ch Eastbury Lass	B	Ch Gentleman Jim	Invincible Belle	J. McNeill	Mrs A. T. Boyes	14.08.44
	Ch Jim's Double of Wychbury	D	Ch Gentleman Jim	Brindle Trix	G. A. Dudley	R. C. Washington	21.12.45
	Ch Lucky Star of Bandits	B	Bucks Mick	Lucy's Luce	E. R. Davis and Mrs. J. F. Gordon	P. K. Boxley	24.06.47
	Ch Monty the Monarch	D	Black Bottle	Willowmay	J. Hudson	T. J. Machin	8.10.44
	Ch Our Queeni	B	Tiger's the Boy	Bombshell Judy	Mrs N. Dunsmuir	F. J. Holloway	15.07.44
	Ch Quiz of Wyncroft	D	Jolly Roger	Gamesters Hot Black	L. Cowgill	A. Bradley	11.05.46
	Ch Wychbury Pied Wonder	B	Ch Widneyland Kim	Quicksilver	G. A. Dudley	R. Willets	30.09.47

Year	Name	Sex	Sire	Dam	Owner	Breeder	Date of Birth
1950	Ch Brinstock Red Radiance	B	Ch Game Laddie	Red Sadie	W. A. Boylan	R. Wilkinson	10.02.46
	Ch Constones Cadet	D	Ch Godfrey's Pride	Constant Coquette	A. W. A. Cairns	A. W. A. Cairns	2.12.48
	Ch Della of Impkin	B	Ch Widneyland Kim	Christie of Wyncroft	Ford and Dady	Mrs. D'arcy Robins	17.10.47
	Ch Godfrey's Pride	D	Ch Widneyland Kim	The Empress Theodora	Ford and Dady	D. F. W. Ford	23.05.47
	Ch Nuneaton Dinah	B	Nuneatonion Boy	Lady Shan	Mrs D. H. Williams	S. Clements	5.01.48
	Ch Peter the Bomber	D	Bomber Command	Pat's the Girl	Mrs E. D. G. Jolly	H. Hatton	31.08.47
	Ch Tawny of Dugarde	B	Ch Sandra's Boy	Jezebel of Dugarde	A. Tryhorn	A. Tryhorn	4.11.48
	Ch Wychbury Kimson	D	Ch Widneyland Kim	Cradley Janet of Wychbury	G. A. Dudley	G. A. Dudley	23.05.47
1951	Ch Emden Corsican	D	Jolly Roger	Emden Clipper	G. C. Henderson	R. Timmins	2.09.45
	Ch Gillcroft Guardson	D	Milkern Guardsman	Lady Patikin	F. Gill	F. Gill	16.09.49
	Ch Goldwyns Leading Lad	D	Wheatley Lad	Brindle Diana	J. A. Altoft	J. A. Altoft	12.01.48
	Ch Nita's Choice	B	Tenacious Pete	Blandona Black	Salisbury & Guest	G. Guest	24.05.47
	Ch Red Atom Bomber	D	Bomber Command	Blackies Girl	F. W. Holden	E. Bradley	26.06.47
	Ch Tearaway Rover	D	Son O'Chall	Troublesom Lass	J. Barnard	H. Fowler	25.05.49
	Ch Tessa's Gem	B	Ch Wychbury Kimbo	Tessa of Burntree	R. V. Tranter	R. V. Tranter	14.09.48
	Ch Widneyland Little Gent of Pynedale	D	Ch Wychbury Kimbo	Pal O'Derek	A. P. Smith	S. Postin	24.10.48
1952	Ch Widneyland Panda	B	Widneyland Little Patch	Brindle Daisy	E. J. Marchant	A. P. Smith	3.04.48
	Ch Chestonian Annoyance	D	Briganda Benbrook Pirate	Beautiful Black Jane	J. Barnard	A. Willets	4.07.49
	Ch Constones Ballyhill Bruce	D	Idol Bruce	Idol Jill	A. W. A. Cairns	A. W. Cooper	14.12.49
	Ch Fancy Fay of Summermuir	B	True Briton	Ch Our Queenie	D. E. A. Meredith	Mrs N. Dunamuir	18.03.49
	Ch Freden Blonde Bombshell	B	Sans Cooper	Perfect Nance	F. W. Holden	F. W. Holden	9.05.51
	Ch Freden Fireworks	D	Sans Cooper	Perfect Nance	R. M. Stevenson	F. W. Holden	1.09.49
	Ch Gwornall Eve	B	Rambling Knight	Gwornall Britannia	H. Bennett	Mrs R. Cartwright	3.05.50
	Ch Lady Cherie of Uddffa	B	Allan's Dynamo	Felicitas of Nunholme	G. W. Bass	G. W. Bass	3.01.49
	Ch Linda of Killyglen	B	Brigands Bo'sun Beau	Colleen of Killyglen	J. McNeill	J. McNeill	5.09.50
	Ch Pal of Aveth CD Ex	D	Ch Quiz of Wyncroft	Elegant Girl	E. H. Payne	G. Guest	23.11.48
	Ch Wychbury Diamond King	D	Diamond Bill	Granby Lass	G. A. Dudley	J. Cherry	13.08.51
1953	Ch Brinstock Welsh Maid	B	Timothy of Dugarde	Queen of Barry	W. A. Boylan	D. Morgan	17.11.50
	Ch Hillside Toby	D	Wishbone Willie	Bourhill Lass	A. J. Wingfield	C. A. Heap	30.09.50

Year	Name	Sex	Sire	Dam	Breeder	Owner	Date
	Ch Little Brindle Queen	B	Ch Widneyland Little Gent of Pynedale	Bonnie Briar	Mrs D. Hoggarth	Mrs D. Hoggarth	17.05.50
1953	Ch Mahogany Democrat	D	Brinstock Democrat	Destructive Meg	A. Fox	W. Kingham	10.01.50
	Ch Red Biddy of Zendiks	B	Brian's Choice	October Lady of Zendiks	Dr J. Silveira	W. M. Morley	29.12.50
1954	Ch Wardonian Corniche	D	Ch Chestonian Annoyance	Wardonian Cintra	J. T. Ward	J. T. Ward	28.09.51
	Ch Wychbury Midly Girl	B	Ch Widneyland Kim	Regnant Show Lady	G. A. Dudley	G. A. Dudley	1.11.51
	Ch Chestonian Satan's Fireworks	D	Ch Freden Fireworks	Barrs Road Pride	J. and T. W. Barnard	F. W. Holden	1.09.51
	Ch Corsair of Wyncole	D	Jolly Roger	Game Lady of Wyncroft	Miss J. D. Peebles	Miss J. D. Peebles	11.05.50
	Ch Emden Cuttysark	D	Ch Godella's Pride	Emden Charanda	Servat & Timmins	Dr P. Lambah	27.08.52
	Ch Gentleman Bruce	D	Crippsian Brindle	Gentle Lady	W. Cutler	Miss J. Blunday	21.11.51
	Ch Godella's Pride	D	Ch Godfrey's Pride	Ch Della of Impkin	Ford and Dady	Ford and Dady	6.04.49
	Ch Gwornall Judith	B	Rambling Knight	Gwornall Britannia	V. A. Johnson	Mrs R. Cartwright	3.05.50
	Ch Wychbury Red Riband	D	Ch Wychbury Kimbo	Regnant Show Lady	G. A. Dudley	G. A. Dudley	24.09.52
	Ch Wychbury Sportsman	D	Ch Widneyland Kim	Primrose Nance	Miss J. M. Cart	R. Heath	1.09.50
	Ch Wyngate Lady	B	Corinthian Rick	Red Demon Lass	R. Walker	G. Miller	25.04.52
	Ch Bellerophon Billy Boy	D	Ch Quiz of Wyncroft	Honest Martha Le Loup	Alan Greenwood	Arnold Greenwood	4.10.53
1955	Ch Challenger of Dugarde	D	Bo'sun of Dugarde	Peggy of Dugarde	A. Tryhorn	A. Tryhorn	1.02.52
	Ch Eastaff Nicola	B	Ch Wychbury Kimbo	Ch Linda of Killyglen	J. McNeill	Miss J. Brightmore	7.12.53
	Ch Fredanseuse	B	Fredante	Apache Princess	F. Baddeley	W. Price	3.03.54
	Ch Goldwyns Gracious Lady	B	Wheatley Lad	Brindle Diana	J. Altoft	J. Altoft	2.12.52
	Ch Lady of Barnfield	B	Ch Thornhill Pride	Fred's Lass of Summermuir	Mrs J. Horsfall	L. Aspin	16.05.51
	Ch Linksbury Derry	B	Ch Godfrey's Pride	Ch Nuneaton Dinah	Mrs D. H. Williams	Mrs D. H. Williams	17.02.51
	Ch Major in Command of Wychbury	D	Ch Wychbury Diamond King	Ch Little Brindle Queen	G. A. Dudley	Mrs D. Hoggarth	7.01.54
	Ch Subtle Difference	D	Ch Widneyland Kim	Model Miss	S. Worrall	S. Worrall	12.12.50
	Ch Tawn Diamond of Dugarde	B	Ch Wychbury Diamond King	Ch Tawney of Dugarde	Mrs D. Hoggarth	A. Tryhorn	18.03.53
	Ch Troglodyte	D	Ch Constones Cadet	Monkswood Menace	B. Yates	Mrs B. Handley	29.09.52
	Ch Williamwood Golden Lass	B	Ch Wychbury Kimbo	Williamwood Wonder Girl	E. R. Judge	E. R. Judge	16.01.52

Year	Name	Sex	Sire	Dam	Owner	Breeder	Date of Birth
1956	Ch Andra of Towans	B	Ch Wychbury Sportsman	Tina of Towans	G. H. Smith	G. H. Smith	16.03.54
	Ch Aphonic True Pal	D	Ch Hillside Toby	Firey Lass	Dean & Roylance	E. Bullough	12.04.53
	Ch Chestonian Elegance	B	Ch Chestonian Annoyance	Ch Freden Blonde Bombshell	J. and T. W. Barnard	J. and T. W. Barnard	25.01.54
	Ch Constones Eastaff This'll do	D	Ch Troglodyte	Jill of Prested	A. W. A. Cairns	Miss J. Brightmore	7.09.54
	Ch Dellveth's Pride	D	Ch Pal of Aveth CD Ex	Dellfrey's Pride	Ford and Dady	Ford and Dady	10.07.53
	Ch Eastaff Danom	D	Ch Goldwyns Leading Lad	Ch Linda of Killyglen	J. McNeill	Miss J. Brightmore	7.08.55
	Ch Golden Boy of Essira	D	Ch Goldwyns Leading Lad	Titian of Dugarde	Mrs N. Weller	N. Weller	20.10.53
	Ch Peter's Boy	D	Ch Peter the Bomber	Brinstock Game 'Un	Mr & Mrs H. R. Wilson	Mrs H. Doncaster	28.02.52
	Ch Smallthorn Brindle Peggy	B	Cheirons Black Mike	Lovely Cottage	S. T. Mansfield	R. Stredwick	27.03.51
	Ch Son of Billy Boy	D	Ch Bellerophon Billy Boy	Little Kip	C. E. Hipwood	C. E. Hipwood	20.08.55
	Ch Weycombe Cherry	B	Gentleman Jackson	Weycombe Judy	G. R. Down	G. R. Down	10.03.54
	Ch Wychbury Sporting Girl	B	Ch Wychbury Sportsman	Saucy Dinah	Mrs J. Horsfall	D. Palmer	25.09.53
1957	Ch Bankhead Beauty	B	Southfield Rufus	Sally Pride of Mayeswood	Mrs E. M. Wylie	Mrs E. M. Wylie	1.10.55
	Ch Linksbury Amanda	B	Linksbury Victor	Ch Linksbury Derry	Mrs D. H. Williams	Mrs D. H. Williams	3.02.53
	Ch Little Diamond Tiara	B	Ch Wychbury Red Riband	Queenie's Dynamite	Mrs D. Hoggarth	Mrs D. Hoggarth	5.06.55
	Ch Trenton Tiger Lily	B	Ch Goldwyns Leading Lad	Deceptive Dora	Mrs H. B. Owen	Mrs H. B. Owen	31.10.52
	Ch Williamwood Fawn Lass	B	Ch Wychbury Red Riband	Ch Williamwood Golden Lass	E. R. Judge	E. R. Judge	23.06.55
1958	Ch Brinstock Glenagow	D	Ch Dellveth's Pride	Ch Brinstock Welsh Maid	W. A. Boylan	Mrs G. W. R. Burge-Smith	26.01.56
	Ch Dennybeck Graftwood Tanya	B	Jupiter of Graftwood	Graftwood Melissande	Mrs J. Horsfall	W. E. Buttler	13.01.56
	Ch Fiona Beauty	B	Crown Major	Ch Gwornall Judith	J. Craig	V. A. Johnson	18.06.55
	Ch Harwyns Choice	D	Kim the Duke	Bill's Baby	T. Roscoe	H. D. Peele	29.07.54
	Ch The Red Brickmaker	D	Ch Wychbury Red Riband	Bilvick Fawn Fixen	T. Batham	T. Batham	4.11.55
		D	Ch Wychbury Diamond Kim	Lady Lesette	L. C. Brown	L. C. Brown	6.06.54
	Ch Toro	B	Ch Wychbury Red Riband	Tina of Towans	G. H. Smith	G. H. Smith	18.03.55

Year	Name	Sex	Sire	Dam	Owner	Breeder	Date
	Ch Towans Merry Maid	B	Ch Wychbury Red Riband	Tina of Towans	G. H. Smith	G. H. Smith	18.03.55
	Ch Wawocan Benita	B	Ch Peter's Boy	Wawocan Little Choice	Latham & Bywater	Latham & Bywater	17.05.56
1959	Ch Buster Bill	D	Ch Bellerophon Billy Boy	Bowbrooke Bess	T. Ward	T. Ward	26.09.56
	Ch Goldwyns Lucky Lad	D	Ch Goldwyns Leading Lad	Ch Goldwyns Gracious Lady	J. Altoft	J. Altoft	12.01.55
	Ch Iron Bill of Phylmajar	D	Ch Peter's Boy	Tinkerbelle Susan	A. D. Thomas	Mr & Mrs H. R. Wilson	12.02.56
	Ch Mandy of Mandalay	B	Ch Godella's Pride	Hayward's Flash	G. Stormont	K. Jones	16.01.56
	Ch Moira Meg	B	Ch Constones Cadet	Nancie's Pride	Mrs E. M. Wylie	C. H. Townsend	10.07.56
	Ch Pitbul Lindy Lou	B	Ch Eastaff Danom	Pitbul Amber Queen	Mrs M. K. Fensom	Mrs M. K. Fensom	9.09.56
	Ch Rellim A'Boy	D	Ch Wychbury Red Riband	Ch Wychbury Midly Girl	Mrs T. Miller	Mrs T. Miller	1.09.57
	Ch Weycombe Dandy	D	Ch Golden Boy of Essira	Ch Weycombe Cherry	Nicolls & Underwood	G. R. Down	30.06.56
	Ch Weycombe Julie	B	Ch Golden Boy of Essira	Ch Weycombe Cherry	A. W. Harkness	G. R. Down	30.06.56
1960	Ch Fredanita of Wychbury	B	Ch Major in Command of Wychbury	Fredansante	Mrs E. M. Myles	E. W. Holden	14.03.58
	Ch Judy of Brunaburgh	E	Ch Bellerophon Billy Boy	Bellerophon Brindle Sue	Dr A. Nugent	Alan Greenwood	16.10.57
	Ch Sahib of Senkrah	D	Ch Eastaff Danom	Ch Weycombe Julie	A. W. Harkness	A. W. Harkness	22.04.58
	Ch Stretfordian Little Gem	B	Stretfordian Lad	Stretfordian Weycombe Trudy	Mrs J. Horsfall	J. Davies	28.04.57
	Ch Weycombe Melody of Senkrah	B	Ch Golden Boy of Essira	Ch Weycombe Cherry	A. W. Harkness	G. R. Down	30.06.56
1961	Ch Brindle Ballerina	B	Ch Major in Command of Wychbury	Lady Black Beauty	Mrs E. E. Hill	L. Harris	13.04.56
	Ch Chestonian Campaign	D	Ch Son of Billy Boy	Maid of Kinderlee	Miss R. J. A. Swindells	H. Simpson	1.07.57
	Ch Fiery Goddess	B	Georgecroft Golden Boy	Satan's Mistress	F. Southall	F. Southall	24.04.58
	Ch Gay Moment	B	Ch Major in Command of Wychbury	Spring Fury	G. Shaw	W. Beasley	5.09.58
	Ch The Prince of Diamonds	D	Ch Major in Command of Wychbury	Lady Flossie of Uddiffa	Mrs V. Johnson	G. W. Bass	12.11.58
	Ch Top Hat	D	Ch Bellerophon Billy Boy	Ruf-E-Nuf of Fulstone	Mr & Mrs A. Eastwood	Mr & Mrs A. Eastwood	12.06.57
	Ch Yasmin of Beredhar	B	Ch Peters Boy	Rivaz of Beredhar	Mrs C. Mercer	R. Cross	26.05.59

Year	Name	Sex	Sire	Dam	Owner	Breeder	Date of Birth
1962	Ch Fredenzella	B	Ch Major in Command of Wychbury	Fredansante	F. W. Holden	F. W. Holden	1.01.60
	Ch Game Penny	B	Weycombe Shan	Glendover Brindle Beverley	A. G. Robbins	A. G. Robbins	17.12.59
	Ch Jolihem Forclip Christy Bella	B	Ch Goldwyns Lucky Lad	Forclip Poor Mary	L. F. Hemstock	D. C. Briggs	15.07.59
	Ch Marjorie's Choice	B	Ch Bellerophon Billy Boy	Dorothy's Choice	K. Whiteley	W. Barnsley	21.10.57
	Ch Rellim Ferryvale Victor	D	Ch Rellim A'Boy	Chestonian Chimes	Mrs T. Miller	F. Ramshaw	8.10.60
	Ch Wynchal Buckeroo	D	Ch Son of Billy Boy	Stanwall Cheeky Charlotte	C. E. Hipwood	C. E. Hipwood	27.06.59
1963	Ch Vesper Andromeda	B	Rumbuster	Vesper Countess	J. Sykes	J. Sykes	16.11.60
	Ch Bandits Brindemara	B	Trenton Colonel	Linksbury Dillyness	P. D. Perry	Mrs D. H. Williams	14.11.61
	Ch Bandits Brintiga	D	Georgecroft Mandumas	Satan's Mistress	T. Field	F. Southall	1.10.59
	Ch Bandits Red Armour	D	Weycombe Gerard	Jill of Bovinger	M. R. Tranter	C. Lowery	1.09.60
	Ch Jolihem Fine and Dandy	D	Jolihem Adonis	Black Fury	Hemstock & Bottomore	C. Bottomore	23.02.61
	Ch Senkrah Saffron	B	Ch Weycombe Dandy	Senkrah Sabelle	S. W. Craik	A. W. Harkness	26.12.60
	Ch Senkrah Sapphire	B	Ch Weycombe Dandy	Senkrah Sabelle	A. W. Harkness	A. W. Harkness	26.12.60
	Ch Stonnards Nell	B	Ch Eastaff Danom	Stonnards Imogen	Mrs B. Cassels	Mrs B. Cassels	10.01.61
	Ch The Black Monarch	D	Black King	Atoms Choice	M. Boam	Barker & Aheme	10.05.59
	Ch Weycombe Benny	D	Weycombe Timothy	Weycombe Beauty	L. H. Lunn	G. R. Down	14.12.57
1964	Ch Freden Dominate	D	Ch The Black Monarch	Ch Fredenzella	F. W. Holden	F. W. Holden	10.06.61
	Ch Game Flash	D	Hydiamond King	Midnight Mischief	A. Baxter	A. Baxter	15.07.61
	Ch Hoplite Red Devil	D	Ainwyn's Redike	Bellerophon Belle Star	T. Rowe	A. Mitchell	9.10.61
	Ch Hyndland Cardinal	D	Hyndland Akela	Williamwood Snow Queen	C. Albrecht	J. Gillespie	16.09.59
	Ch Jolihem El Toro	D	Bankhead Bullet	Ch Mandy of Mandalay	L. F. Hemstock	G. J. Stormost	2.03.62
	Ch Monkhill Candy	B	Rumbuster	Wynchal Bluebell	F. Randall	F. Randall	13.11.62
	Ch Pitbul Sally Ann	B	Winterfold Danny	Widneyland Pitbul Lassie	K. Fenson	K. Fenson	31.08.60
	Ch Regency Gal	B	Rumbuster	Clear Brew	F. Randall	R. E. Salisbury	1.06.62
	Ch Senkrah Sabutae	B	Ch Weycombe Dandy	Senkrah Sabelle	Mrs T. Miller	A. W. Harkness	23.09.62
	Ch The Red Battler	D	The Red Avenger	Kentucky Sue	G. Rogers	E. S. Ward	17.02.61
	Ch Wirswall Betsy	B	Admiral Albert	Rhodesian Ch Stanestreet Glenbriar	Mrs E. M. Myles	Mrs E. M. Myles	16.01.60

Year	Name	Sex	Sire	Dam	Breeder	Owner	Date
1965	Ch Wychcombe Rob's Pride	B	Ch Weycombe Benny	Ch Game Penny	A. G. Robbins	A. G. Robbins	5.05.61
	Ch Camdonain Contender	D	Ch Rellim Ferryvale Victor	Ch Game Penny	Miss K. G. and M. E. Morris	A. G. Robbins	23.12.62
	Ch Dennybeck Dani of Belsivore	B	Ch Eastaff Danom	Dennybeck Dinkum	Mesdames P. M. and D. M. Holmes	Mrs. J. Horsfall	18.08.63
	Ch Dyrex Duskie Belle	B	Hydiamond King	Dyrex Fair Jayne	D. J. Wilkes	D. J. Wilkes	28.10.62
	Ch Hyndland Jaunty Jock	D	Ch Eastaff Danom	Hyndland Cherry	M. Gillespie and G. Stevenson	F. and G. Gillespie	3.02.63
	Ch Kinderlee Cavalcade	B	Ch Son of Billy Boy	Ch Brindle Ballerina	Mrs G. Gallimore	Mrs E. E. Hill	15.09.61
	Ch Rapparee Ashfield Star	B	Boy Pat	Padarn Rosebud	Mr & Mrs J. Bolton	E. Brown	18.08.62
	Ch Sanville Wild Puma	B	Saracen of Senkrah	Sanville Wild Maid	W. Watson	W. Watson	16.12.62
	Ch Senkrah Sabeau	B	Ch Weycombe Dandy	Senkrah Sabelle	R. McEvoy	A. W. Harkness	26.12.60
	Ch Walstaff Domino	D	Black King	Walstaff Midnight Tina	G. W. Walton	G. W. Walton	10.05.60
1966	Ch. William the Conqueror	D	Winterfold Danny	Gentle Tamsie	Miss J. Crew	T. Hanks	10.10.61
	Ch Buninyong Caesar	D	Ch Weycombe Dandy	Frolicking Flip	H. Folkes	Mr & Mrs B. Wiltshire	7.08.64
	Ch Constones Compact	B	Bankhead Benjamin	Constones Comette	Mr & Mrs A. M. Lee	A. W. A. Cairns	5.09.63
	Ch Curfews White Orchid	B	Ch Eastaff Danom	Ch Orchid Beauty	F. J. Clark	V. Pounds	7.03.65
	Ch Famous Lad of Wirswall	D	Ch The Black Monarch	Wirswall Duchess	Mrs E. M. Myles and C. Townsend	Mrs. E. M. Myles	9.06.63
	Ch Freden Bothered	B	Ch The Black Monarch	Ch Fredenzella	N. Edwards	F. W. Holden	15.06.63
	Ch Jolihem Black Beauty	B	Ch Jolihem El Toro	Jolihem Sabelle	L. F. Hemstock	L. F. Hemstock	25.04.64
	Ch Jolihem Dreadnought	D	Ch Eastaff Danom	Jolihem Nuncargate Josie	L. F. Hemstock	L. F. Hemstock	14.06.64
	Ch Knight Templar	D	Ch Rellim Ferryvale Victor	Ch Marjorie's Choice	K. Whiteley	K. Whiteley	5.02.63
	Ch Lydes Cygnet	B	Ch Rellim Ferryvale Victor	Linksbury Derry Dhu	Mrs M. C. Hughes	Mrs M. C. Hughes	18.10.63
	Ch Pitbul Colleen	B	Ch Eastaff Danom	Pitbull Amber Princess	Mr & Mrs K. Fensom	Mrs. M. K. Fensom	9.09.61
1967	Ch Badgerlea Biddy	B	Ch Eastaff Danom	Ch Senkrah Saffron	S. W. Craik	S. W. Craik	20.12.63
	Ch Brindis Kim	B	Brindis Jaguar	Brindis Juno	M. Hoban	Mr & Mrs W. Atkinson	30.11.63
	Ch Gwynford Drumbeat	D	Ch Game Flash	Gwynford Winter Witch	F. Burford	F. Burford	13.07.63
	Ch Jasper of Witts	D	Ch Eastaff Danom	Lass of Nutgrove	S. Bartlett	S. Bartlett	12.10.64
	Ch Kinderlee Cashelle	B	Irish Ch Thoroak Sorrel Sam	Int. Ch Senkrah Sabeau	Mrs. E. E. Hill	R. McEvoy	4.05.65
	Ch Orchid Beauty	B	Ch Brinstock Glenagow	Black Orchid	V. H. Pounds	V. H. Pounds	21.12.62

Year	Name	Sex	Sire	Dam	Owner	Breeder	Date of Birth
	Ch Rapparee Renegade	D	Ch Game Flash	Walstaff Tigre Tigrato	Mr & Mrs J. Bolton	S. Bennett	7.10.64
	Ch Relim Warpaint	D	Ch Rellim Ferryvale	Ch Senkrah Sabutae	G. Down	Mrs T. Miller	21.10.65
	Ch Rossisle Rivorich Maxmillion	D	Ch Chestonian Campaign	Freden Beguiled	Miss R. J. A. Swindells and C. A. Smith	J. Talbot	9.06.64
1968	Ch Sanville Wild Clover	B	Weycombe Shan	Senkrah Wild Maid	W. E. Burrows	W. Watson	21.08.64
	Ch Badgerlea Rascal	B	Ch Eastaff Danom	Ch Senkrah Saffron	Craik and Howarth	S. W. Craik	28.08.65
	Ch Dennybeck Brindis Liqueur	B	Dennybeck Diamond King	Dennybeck Delight	Mrs P. Brooks	Mr & Mrs W. Atkinson	8.12.63
	Ch Linksbury Augustus	D	Trenton Colonel	Linksbury Mairi	Mrs J. Fisher	Mrs J. Fisher	27.08.63
	Ch Lydes Winston Defiant	D	Ch Jolihem El Toro	Freden De Lovely	Mrs S. M. Fox	Mrs M. C. Hughes	30.11.64
	Ch Rossisle Hobson	D	Ch Chestonian Campaign	Rossisle Fredenina	Miss R. J. A. Swindells and C. A. Smith	Miss R. J. A. Swindells and C. A. Smith	30.03.63
	Ch Sanville Wild Cheetah	B	Saracen of Senkrah	Senkrah Wild Maid	W. Watson	W. Watson	16.12.62
	Ch Topcroft Temptress	B	Ch Bandits Brintiga	Topcroft Tar Baby	Mr & Mrs E. J. Bywaters	H. Latham	27.11.65
	Ch Topcroft Toreador	D	Ch Bandits Brintiga	Topcroft Tar Baby	H. Latham	H. Latham	27.11.65
	Ch Wirswall Jet the Monarch	D	Ch The Black Monarch	Georgeous Gusie of Wirswall	Mrs E. M. Myles and M. Boam	Mrs E. M. Myles	19.12.65
1969	Ch Battlers Pop-Along-a-Bit	B	Ch The Red Battler	Nuzwig Kanga	A. G. Phillips	H. M. Tynesley	6.03.64
	Ch Benext Beauty Be	B	Gwen's Danny Boy	Benext Pamarandy Christabella	Mr & Mrs K. Bailey	Mr & Mrs. K. Bailey	27.07.64
	Ch Benext Beau	D	Ulsterville Major	Ch Benext Beauty Be	Mr & Mrs K. Bailey	Mr & Mrs. K. Bailey	20.01.67
	Ch Christopher of Geneva	D	Admiral Robert	Sisao Lubby Lou	Mrs R. Williams	Mrs M. Earwaker	25.12.63
	Ch Dennybeck Eliza Doolitle	B	Dennybeck Hard Diamond	Dennybeck Drum Girl	Mrs P. Brooks	Mrs J. Horsfall	12.11.66
	Ch Durward Demon	B	Irish Ch Raynan Dandy	Irish Ch Weycombe Venessa	Harkness & Dunn	R. McEvoy	2.01.65
	Ch Jolihem Gallant Bess	B	Ch Jolihem Dreadnought	Hillstaffs Lucky Gem	L. F. Hemstock	Mrs J. Pellington	4.02.68
	Ch Jubilant of Jolihem	D	Ch Jolihem El Toro	Jolihem Isabella	G. Goddard	L. F. Hemstock	27.04.63
	Ch Kinderlee Critique	B	Ch Topcroft Toreador	Kinderlee Cambrian	H. Latham and Mrs E. E. Hill	Mr & Mrs A. K. Hill	1.07.68
	Ch Langport Spearhead	D	Ch Freden Dominate	Rossisle Marquita	K. C. Langdon	H. V. Langdon	2.03.67
	Ch Rapparee Threapwood Handyman	D	Ch Rapparee Renegade	Betchgreen Blacklass	Mr. & Mrs. J. Bolton and H. W. Clamp	Mrs A. Banks	4.09.67
	Ch Red Kim	D	Bantam Boy	Dennybeck Drum Girl	Mrs E. P. Stark	A. Thackray	14.08.64
	Ch Red Zarni	D	Rebel Man	Miss Penny Packer	Mrs D. M. Woodward	P. Parkes	20.07.66
	Ch Sanville Red Dawn	B	The Young Pretender	Ch Sanville Wild Cheetah	W. Watson	W. Watson	12.11.67

Year	Name	Sex	Sire	Dam	Breeder	Owner	Date
	Ch Wystaff Warfare	D	Kinderlee Commando	Wystaff Rossisle Rosina	Mr & Mrs R. Armitage	Mrs G. Gallimore	20.01.66
1970	Ch Gamestock Bonnie of Burns	B	Jack of Spades	Dark Castle Lass	P. Jepson	B. Bradley	14.05.67
	Ch Hambrea Super Flash	D	Ch Game Flash	Fulfin Firefly	H. J. Wall	Mr & Mrs A. Hammersley	8.09.65
	Ch Jumping Bean of Grenoside	B	Ch Topcroft Toreador	Grenoside Honey Bee	C. H. Senior	W. W. Greaves	27.08.67
	Ch Rainsbrook Renegade	D	Mountainash Xmas Titan	Rainsbrook Trial Edition	J. Bamber	Mrs D. Parker	15.06.67
	Ch Rapparee Roulette	B	Ch Jolihem Dreadnought	Ch Rapparee Ashfield Star	Mr & Mrs J. Bolton	Mr & Mrs J. Bolton	1.09.65
	Ch Rossisle Alverthorpe Dark Judy	B	Red Fury	Dark Eyed Kim	Miss R. J. A. Swindells	T. Cunnane	19.09.64
1971	Ch Ashstock Artful Bess	B	Ch Camdonian Contender	Barrington Wild Rose	Mr & Mrs A. A. Waters	Mr & Mrs A. A. Waters	18.04.68
	Ch Blakens Dark Prospect	E	Ch Wystaff Warfare	Blaken's Battlers	A. G. Phillips	A. G. Phillips	7.01.69
	Ch Brocliffe Brindis U Like	E	Dennybeck Hard Diamond	Dennybeck Delight	Mrs J. Horsfall	Mr & Mrs Atkinson	2.10.68
	Ch Buccaneer Shoemaker	D	Ch Topcroft Toreador	Bridgehouse Sandpiper	A. Johnson	W. Sheeny	20.03.69
	Ch Hoplite Fearless Devil	D	Hoplite Horniman	Hoplite Hussy	W. McNight	A. Mitchell	2.02.67
	Ch Jolihem Ringmaster	D	Ch Jolihem Dreadnought	Hillstaff's Lucky Gem	L. F. Hemstock	Mrs J. Pellington	4.02.68
	Ch Rapparee Look Lively	D	Hydiamond King	Rapparee Lady Luck	L. Barnett	Mr & Mrs J. Bolton	20.04.67
	Ch Rapparee Rothersyke Vow	D	Ch Rapparee Threapwood Handyman	Rothersyke Gem	Mr & Mrs J. Bolton	Dr I. W. Davidson	6.06.69
	Ch Sanville Red Rhapsody	B	Senkrah Sabre	Ch Sanville Wild Cheetah	G. A. Dudley	W. Watson	18.11.68
	Ch Satan's Master	D	Ch Topcroft Toreador	Kinderlee Conchita	K. J. Boyham	Mrs B. Topping	19.05.69
	Ch Staffshaven Artificer	D	Ch Topcroft Toreador	Badgerlea Kate	Mrs J. R. Bennett	Mrs J. R. Bennett	8.09.68
	Ch Torosay Black Fern	B	Ch Bandits Brintiga	Torosay Masterpiece	D. Gilmour	Dr. C. MacLean	8.09.67
	Ch Wawocan Jezebel	B	Wawocan Buccaneer	Ch Popcroft Temptress	Mr & Mrs E. J. Bywaters	Mr & Mrs E. J. Bywaters	16.01.68
	Ch Yennips Sarabelle	B	Mountainash Xmas Atlas	Countrymans Coppice	Mr & Mrs W. Todd	R. P. Henshaw	4.11.66
1972	Ch Gadet's Last Chance	B	Ch Rapparee Look	Buccaneer Penny	T. Fury	A. Johnson	11.03.71
	Ch Ginnels Moonlight Madonna	B	Chestonian Arrogant	Liam's Gire	W. E. Jones	W. E. Jones	3.02.69
	Ch Highland Squire	D	Sanville Red Warrior	Cheshire Brandy	J. Stirling	D. T. Reid	14.02.69
	Ch Langport Avenger	D	Ch Gwynford Drumbeat	Langport Solitaire Queen	H. V. Langdon	H. V. Langdon	2.04.70

Year	Name	Sex	Sire	Dam	Owner	Breeder	Date of Birth
	Ch Rapparee Grand Slam	B	Larujon Leader	Rapparee Razzle Dazzle	Mr & Mrs. J. Bolton	Mr & Mrs. J. Bolton	26.01.70
	Ch Rellim Saratoga Skiddy	B	Ch Rellim Ferryvale Victor	Rellim Fenella	Mrs T. Miller	Mrs T. Miller	22.10.68
	Ch Rockmere Rip-it-up	D	Sanville Red Ranger	Rockmere Vemport Shina	Mr & Mrs J. R. McKellar	Mr & Mrs J. R. McKellar	4.07.69
	Ch Rothersyke Maid	B	Larujon Leader	Calderbrig Carmen	Dr & Mrs. I. W. Davidson	Dr & Mrs I. W. Davidson	5.10.67
	Ch Ruadh of Hawkslee	B	Sanville Wild Beaver	Lass of Senkrah	D. R. Grant	D. Weston	1.09.67
1973	Ch Barrington Golden Toga	B	Ch Buninyong Caesar	Barrington Rellim Regina	Miss P. Machaglan	Major and Mrs. Rowley and Miss Anderson	16.02.67
	Ch Comstones Grim Girl	B	Ch Freden Dominate	Ch Comstones Compact	Mr & Mrs W. Alexander	Lee & Cairns	16.05.69
	Ch Durwood Deodante	D	Rellim Billy Bow	Flora of Stockwell	Mr & Mrs I. Dunn	Mrs Campbell	2.02.71
	Ch Elegance of Sanville	B	Print of Wyncole	Sanville Red Enchantress	Prentice & Watson	W. Watson	14.09.69
	Ch Meaduns Polly Flinders	B	Ch Rapparee Rothersyke Vow	Somerset Sheila	H. A. Dunn	J. Evans	1.11.70
	Ch Mill Lass of Judael	B	Mat of Stainlaw	Janine of Judael	Searle & Earle	M. Searle	18.08.69
	Ch Moi Daredevil	D	Ch Rapparee Rothersyke Vow	Moi Carousel	J. J. Dibling	K. Layland	21.10.70
	Ch Quite Contrary of Rapparee	B	Ch Rapparee Rothersyke Vow	Dusky Maid	Mr & Mrs J. Bolton	R. Martin	17.02.72
	Ch Rapparee The Gladiator	D	Larujon Leader	Rapparee Razzle Dazzle	Mr & Mrs A. Sparks	Mr & Mrs J. Bolton	26.01.70
	Ch Reetuns Lord Jim	D	Ch Rapparee Threapwood Handyman	Elvinor Miranda	Messrs Wood and Holmes	A. Wood	20.04.72
	Ch Sanville Red Ember	B	Senkrah Sabre	Ch Sanville Wild Cheetah	J. G. Porteus	W. Watson	18.11.68
	Ch Wawocan Kinsman	D	Ch Topcroft Toreador	Ch Topcroft Temptress	Mrs M. Graham	Mr & Mrs. E. J. Bywater	2.03.69
1974	Ch Ashstock Black Maria	B	Ch Rapparee Rothersyke Vow	Ch Ashstock Artful Bess	Mr & Mrs A. Waters	Mr & Mrs A. Waters	11.04.72
	Ch Ashstock Max the Miller	D	Dennybeck Hard Diamond	Ch Ashstock Artful Bess	Mr & Mrs A. Waters	Mr. & Mrs. A. Waters	13.01.71
	Ch Betchgreen Sheena	B	Ch Rapparee The Gladiator	Betchgreen Flashless	W. Hodgkinson	W. Hodgkinson	24.05.71
	Ch Brocliffe Best Bet	B	Kinderlee Cobra	Ch Dennybeck Eliza Doolittle	Mrs P. Brookes	Mrs. P. Brookes	24.04.71
	Ch Cardinal Sin of Beaconmoor	D	Verles Viceroy	Asbury Mulla	Mr & Mrs M. Mitchell	Mrs G. Ormonde	20.02.72
	Ch Cradbury Flash	B	Ch Rapparee Rothersyke V...	Cradbury Lady Flash	F. A. Phillips	F. A. Phillips	27.05.72

Year	Name	Sex	Sire	Dam			Date
	Ch Dark Rose of Topcroft	B	Ch West Point Warrior	Topcraft Caprice	Mr & Mrs W. Bennett	Messrs Latham and Rickard	31.07.71
	Ch Lunar Flash	D	Ch Rapparee Look Lively	Perky Ellen	Mr & Mrs Fern	A. W. Skett	10.07.69
	Ch Pitbul Jeff's Pal	D	Ch Jolihem Dreadnought	Pitbul Christabelle	Mr & Mrs W. Jones	Mr & Mrs K. Fensom	1.02.69
	Ch Redeal Mik	D	Ch Satan's Master	Mistress Sheba	J. Leader	J. Leader	13.05.70
	Ch Red Rapture of Hamason	B	Ch Rockmere Rip-it-Up	Sanville Red Rhapsody	Mr & Mrs Robinson	G. A. Dudley	7.05.72
	Ch Spotty Lady	B	Ch Rapparee Look Lively	Buccaneer Penny Black	C. Whitworth	A. Johnson	11.03.71
	Ch Westpoint Warrior	D	Ch Topcroft Toreador	Owd Bett	A. McDermott	W. Whitehurst	8.09.69
	Ch Yennips Golden	D	Mountainash Xmas Titan	Towans Mia Petite Ami	Mr & Mrs. F. Ward	Mr & Mrs. W. Todd	6.04.70
1975	Ch Ashmoss Billy's Girl of Valgo	B	Son of Templar	Black Orchid of Touchstone	Mr & Mrs G. Golding	J. Acton	28.10.72
	Ch Ashstock Brinchester	D	Dennybeck Hard Diamond	Ch Ashstock Artful Bess	Mr & Mrs. E. Skeets	Mr & Mrs A. Waters	13.01.71
	Ch Cradbury Lord Vow	D	Ch Rapparee Rothersyke Vow	Lady of Verona	R. D. H. Gittins	M. Gwilt	14.07.73
	Ch Durward Dorlesa	B	Kimbrook of Suffolk	Danville Red Sparkler	M. Currie	I. Dunn	22.02.72
	Ch Jokartan Royal Tan	D	Ch Jolihem Ringmaster	Brocliffe Bountiful	J. Argie	J. Argie	30.06.73
	Ch Kerrisdale Orchids Fancy	B	Trebblo Little Fella	Kerrisdale Little Miss Cinders	V. H. Pounds	Mrs A. Gatenby	4.01.73
	Ch Kerrisdale Tufnut of Raan	B	Trebblo Little Fella	Kerrisdale Little Miss Cinders	Mr & Mrs R. Blackmore	Mrs A. Gatenby	4.01.73
	Ch Linda of Tinkinswood	B	Brombill Chief Stoker	Bonny Queen	T. Fletcher	P. E. Lewis	22.11.71
	Ch Midnight Riot	D	Ch Rothersyke Vow	Rapparee Riot Belle	Mrs P. Carless	B. Corbett	12.02.72
	Ch Reetuns Aristocrat	D	Ch Westpoint Warrior	Elinor Miranda	Mrs T. Ward	A. Wood	26.09.73
	Ch Rossisle Trump Card	B	Satchmo Goodliness	Ch Rossisle Alverthorpe Dark Judy	Mrs R. J. A. Swindells	Mrs. R. J. A. Swindells	18.07.72
	Ch Staffs McMichael	D	Burntwoods Red Devil	Dark-eyed Sandra	L. Berry	J. Larkin	27.11.71
	Ch Tom Crib of Sparpit	D	Livstaff Black Knight	Dusky Maid	Mr & Mrs A. Sparks	A. Burrows	29.04.73
	Ch Vencristo Ambience	B	Brindis Ultimate	Elvinor Westwards Bess	N. Entwistle	N. Entwistle	19.04.72
1976	Ch Anjemag Aussie	D	Bertjen Jordanhill Rebel	Senkrah Sanell	Mr & Mrs A. Humphreys and A. Harkness	Mr & Mrs A. Humphreys	15.09.73
	Ch Ashstock Lucky Jim	D	Ch Rapparee Rothersyke Vow	Ch Ashstock Artful Bess	Mr & Mrs A. Devlin	Mr & Mrs A. Waters	11.04.72
	Ch Ashstock Red Buttons	B	Ashstock Thornhill Prince	Ashstock Iron Peg	Mr & Mrs W. G. Dew	Mr & Mrs. A. Waters	6.07.73

Year	Name	Sex	Sire	Dam	Owner	Breeder	Date of Birth
	Ch Boggarts Black Pearl	B	Ruffhill Brindle Basher	Keencluff Carousel	L. B. Walker	L. Barnett	13.02.73
	Ch Bronco Morning Light	B	Ch Rapparee the Gladiator	Sparpit Sea Sprite	Mr & Mrs. J. Webley	Mr & Mrs. J. Webley	16.01.74
	Ch Hamason Red Rambler	D	Sanville Red Ranger	Dark Demon Lass of Hamason	Mr & Mrs H. Robins	Mr & Mrs H. Robins	11.10.74
	Ch Hurricane of Judael	D	Sheila's Little Skipper	Crisp of Judael	Mr & Mrs J. E. Pringle	M. Searle and G. Earle	27.06.74
	Ch Moekens Cyclone	D	Dumbriton Baldie Thompson	Swinfen Sunflower	J. Dunn	Mr & Mrs K. Brown	1.07.74
	Ch St Simon's Argonaut	D	Ch Westpoint Warrior	Sanbryn Comedy	Mrs P. Hayes	G. M. Grosvenor	19.02.72
	Ch Sparpit Lavender Liz	B	Livstaff Black Knight	Pit Rose	Mr & Mrs A. Sparks	Mr & Mrs. A. Sparks	10.10.74
	Ch Swinfen Sky Scraper	D	Brindis Ultimate	Dennybeck Diehard	Mr & Mrs H. Gudgeon	S. Saul	6.03.71
	Ch Thorndyke White Miracle	D	Janesen Boy	Thorndyke Jane	E. Dyke	E. Dyke	2.08.74
1977	Ch Carn Dearg Ne'erday	B	Dunbriton Baldie Thompson	Durward Dusty Dinah	Mr & Mrs I. MacEachern	Mr & Mrs I. MacEachern	1.01.74
	Ch Cap Coch Whiplash	D	Fighting Mike	Cap Coch Tuti Fruti	K. W. Horwood	W. Oakley	3.03.75
	Ch Deistar of Durward	B	Ch Tom Crib of Sparpit	Maromen Attar of Minx	Mr & Mrs I. Dunn	Mr & Mrs H. Kennedy	22.02.75
	Ch Ellestere Bella	B	Commanche Thunderflash	Steveleen's Judy	Mr & Mrs A. Rowe	Mr & Mrs S. Kelly	9.10.72
	Ch Gamestock Love Bug of Cubik	B	Buckhill Black Bomber	Buckhill Hostess	Mrs J. Ashburner	P. Jepson	8.11.71
	Ch Glenrhondda Sombrebell of Dogan	B	Ch Westpoint Warrior	Isengard Patsy	B. Cadogan and A. Thomas	Mrs G. Thomas	2.09.74
	Ch Hamason Red Radiance	B	Ch Hamason Red Rambler	Ch Red Rapture of Hamason	Mr & Mrs H. Robinson	Mr & Mrs. H. Robinson	28.08.75
	Ch Kinderdijk Petite Cherie	B	Ch Pitbul Jeff's Pal	Hot Chocolate	Mr & Mrs R. Astley	Mr & Mrs W. E. Sadler	22.09.74
	Ch Moekens Whirlwind	B	Dunbriton Baldie Thompson	Swinfen Sunflower	Mr & Mrs. K. Brown	Mr & Mrs. K. Brown	1.07.74
	Ch Pitbul Red Regent	D	Irish Ch Ban Ri of Cuileog	Pitbul Bullwip Ebony Princess	Mr & Mrs K. Fensom	Mr & Mrs. K. Fensom	10.11.75
	Ch Pitfighta Dark Duke	D	Ch Langport Avenger	Ch Constones Grim Girl	Mr & Mrs W. Alexander	Mr & Mrs W. Alexander	10.03.75
	Ch Rocketeer Nancy Girl	B	Ch Redeal Mik	Vrondeg Flash	Mr & Mrs B. Noon	Mr & Mrs G. Parry	18.08.74
	Ch Rumbow Black Bess	B	Ch Rapparee the Gladiator	Wiley Dark Rose	A. E. Jones	W. Till	7.02.74
	Ch Tenax Trampas	D	Brocliffe Best Bitter	Tenax Touch of Gold	J. Gibson	J. Gibson	29.11.74

Year	Name	Sex	Sire	Dam	Owner	Breeder	Date of Birth
	Ch Durward Dark Dancer	B	Ch Durward Deodante	Ch Delstar of Durward	Mr & Mrs I. Dunn	Mr & Mrs I. Dunn	2.06.78
	Ch Goldwyn Leading Star	B	Ch Red Rum	Star Prize	Mr & Mrs P. Wall	Mr & Mrs P. Wall	27.04.78
	Ch Maratonger Rip Rap	D	Gypsy Daniels of Sparpit	Maratongers Bess's Girl	G. Byrne	G. Byrne	31.10.75
1980	Ch Meaduns Cleopatra	B	Ruffhill Showboy	Meaduns Marie Antonette	H. A. Dunn	H. A. Dunn	26.02.76
	Ch Red Rum	D	Vencristo Domino	Vencristo Amber	Mr & Mrs T. Ruddie	Mr & Mrs T. Ruddie	20.07.76
	Ch Rendorn no Retreat	B	Brewmaster Sparticus	Rendorn Regal Flash	N. Berry	N. Berry	20.11.77
	Ch Scarthwaite Temptress	B	Royal Duke of Scarthwaite	Eshbee Beauty of Scarthwaite	L. Aspin	L. Aspin	16.08.75
	Ch Skean Dhu	D	Ch Black Tusker	Constones Paragon	G. Carter	Mrs P. B. Grotrain	24.04.78
1981	Ch Duchess of Aubrey	B	Ch Rapparee Rothersyke Vow	Honey End Bess	M. Burke	Mrs Bishop	10.08.78
	Ch Evaredee Sergeant Pepper	B	Sir Sous Nox	The Foundling	Mr & Mrs M. J. Homan	J. Peters	7.07.76
	Ch Ginnels Black Tuskyanna	D	Ch Black Tusker	Ginnels Madonnas Moon Maid	Mr & Mrs P. Shoulder	W. E. Jones	10.12.78
	Ch Jolaine Wild Gypsy	E	Livstaff Black Knight	Mosscroft Kimbella	Mrs J. Eva	Mr & Mrs J. Cooper	28.10.77
	Ch Karjobri Black Pepper	E	Ch Black Tusker	Karjobri Precious Lass	Mr & Mrs B. Grattidge	Mr & Mrs B. Grattidge	17.11.77
	Ch Lawbury Cadiz Kid	E	Ch Pitfighta Dark Blue	Hazelberry Go-Go	Mr & Mrs V. & T. Lawlor	Mr & Mrs V. & T. Lawlor	2.06.78
	Ch Netherionion Tweedle-Dee-De	B	Betchgreen Dubber	Ruffhill Queenie	Mr & Mrs G. Westwood	W. Beasley	19.10.77
	Ch Pegs Bolton Trip	D	Ch Hurricane of Judael	Sharnford Black Diamond	J. E. Pringle	R. A. Henry	5.12.78
	Ch Pitmax The Matador	D	Ch Swinfen Skyscraper	Lady Red Samba	R. W. Harper	P. Shelley	30.08.77
	Ch Red Prince of Hamason	D	Hamason Red Rajah	Powerstown Susie	J. W. Ratcliffe	J. Ford	23.09.77
	Ch Whitebury Crown	D	Brijon Battle Hymn	Ch Boggarts Black Pearl	H. Ward	P. Walker	24.06.77
	Ch Worden Queen	D	Benjamin Worden Lad	Ch Acid Queen	Mrs M. M. Gilfoyle	M. Green	10.10.78
1982	Ch Baroness of Bettandy	B	Ch Hurricane of Judael	Pitmax Hot Ember	Mr & Mrs F. Saunders	Mr & Mrs Whelan	31.05.80
	Ch Bens Renegade of Baracane	D	Baracane Midnight Marauder	Jephson Jane	J. & B. J. Munro	V. White	23.09.80

Year	Name	Sex	Sire	Dam	Breeder	Owner	Date
	Ch Touch and Go of Beaconmoor	B	Verless Viceroy	Tyrannus Belle	Mrs F. MacMillan	Miss A. Rogers	24.08.73
1978	Ch Acid Queen	B	Ch Hurricane of Judael	Jinny Arenskaya	M. J. Green	Mrs J. Plowes	6.01.76
	Ch Alpaka Lolas Dream	B	Royal Duke of Scarthwaite	Alpaka Bobs Fancy	Mr & Mrs A. S. Tittle	Mr & Mrs A. S. Tittle	17.07.73
	Ch Black Tusker	D	Black King	Lady Bella Madonna	B. Bates and M. Boam	G. Cowdell	8.10.75
	Ch Cottfol Princess of Tridwr	B	Irish Ch Carivale Conquestor	Fawn Fury	T. Fletcher	Cotter & Foley	1.06.76
	Ch Eastern Star of Zilabra	B	Zilabra Son of Squire	Zilabra Miss Nippy	Dewar & McKinnon	Mrs M. Graham	23.11.72
	Ch Frolbeca Fireraiser	D	Jolihem Ringmaster	Iron Porsche	Mr & Mrs C. H. Green	F. Sweeney	22.09.72
	Ch Rendorn Deadly Nightshade	B	Ch Hurricane of Judael	Rendorn Rapid Reprisal	N. Berry	N. Berry	6.09.76
	Ch Scarthwaite Coachman	D	Royal Duke of Scarthwaite	Eshbee Beauty of Scarthwaite	L. Aspin	L. Aspin	16.08.75
1979	Ch Anglestaff Blue Max	D	Benext Begin of Anglestaff	Kerrisdale Debbie Bess	Mr & Mrs A. and C. Carlini	Mr & Mrs A. and C. Carlini	4.06.77
	Ch Bobon Amber Gambler	B	Ch Moekens Cyclone	Moekens Onyx	Mr & Mrs A. Bloomfield	Mr & Mrs A. Bloomfield	26.06.77
	Ch Kaluki Duke	D	Warlock of Rothersyke	Cradbury Flash Gem	Mr & Mrs G. Dickens	Messrs R. and P. Benson	22.10.75
	Ch Kandon Brindle Ben	D	Ruffhill the Midlander	Netheronian Saucey Girl	Mr & Mrs P. Lloyd	Mr & Mrs Westwood	28.09.77
	Ch Little Miss Kek	B	Ch Hurricane of Judael	Velvet Queen	Mr & Mrs Green	Mr & Mrs Green	2.11.76
	Ch Mac Shiehallion	D	Ch Hurricane of Judael	Red Kate	Mrs J. Short	M. Kinsley	5.07.76
	Ch Meaduns Emma Hamilton	B	Ruffhill Showboy	Ch Meaduns Polly Flinders	H. A. Dunn	H. A. Dunn	26.05.76
	Ch Montbell Barbarossa	D	Ch Pitbul Red Regent	Ch Ashstock Red Buttons	Mr & Mrs J. G. Bird	Mr & Mrs Drew	12.02.77
	Ch Shepstaff Black Pearl	B	Raphael's Black Ace	Westbourne Brindle Plague	Mrs B. H. Buxton	Mr & Mrs Shepherd	11.01.75
	Ch Sundow Swashbuckler	D	Briton Battle Hymn	Kelba of Kinderlee	Mr & Mrs G. R. Pearson	Mr & Mrs G. R. Pearson	25.01.77
	Ch Tapstaff Samantha of Chalfont	B	Torcrest Ambassador	Tapstaff Beauty	Mrs P. A. Painter	R. G. Bradshaw	14.09.73
1980	Ch Bracken of Judael	B	Highmoor Dandy of Judael	Gold Pride of Judael	J. B. Preston	M. Searle and G. Earle	20.07.78
	Ch Briglen Arcturus	B	Ch Scarthwaite Coachman	Briglen Adversary	Mr & Mrs B. Whitehouse	Mr & Mrs B. Whitehouse	13.02.78
	Ch Brocliffe Benjamin	D	Carivale Double Century	Ch Brocliffe Best Bet	E. R. Donnley	Mrs P. Brooks	16.11.76

	Sex					Date
Ch Bodjer of Kenstaff	D	Mercian Turque	Miriam of Mercia	Mr & Mrs F. Gough	M. D. & Y. S. Henderson	10.02.77
Ch Earlsdon Viceroy of Benfirth	D	Ch Black Tusker	Earlsdon Spitfire	D. J. & E. M. Bentley	Mr & Mrs J. D. Bocth	14.05.81
Ch Maradin Master Mariner	D	Betchgreen Dubber	Bethane Bitter Sweet	Mrs E. Bradford	Mrs E. Bradford	28.10.79
Ch Pitmax Pasidion of Dumbriton	D	Ch Red Rum	Lady Red Samba	D. Gilmour	P. Shelley	6.11.79
Ch Redstaff King	D	Ch Jokartan Royal Tan	Pitmax Brazen Lady	H. Doughty	W. J. Pearson	27.07.79
Ch Rendorn Devils Timpani	B	Ch Black Tusker	Ch Rendorn No Retreat	N. Berry	N. Berry	19.11.80
Ch Rocellio Miss Supreme	B	Goldwyn Golden Lad	Rocellio Belle Star	Mr & Mrs R. Pugh	Mr & Mrs R. Pugh	7.09.80
Ch Solo Gypsy Fiddler	B	Ch Karjobri Black Pepper	Purdy Prima Donna	R. Wint	R. Wint	24.08.80
Ch Szelyng Uno Who	B	Ruffhill the Midlander	Szelyng Harrys Choice	Mr P. Wilkinson & Mrs S. Goode	Mr P. Wilkinson & Mrs S. Goode	25.01.80

The Kennel Club

Champions (Show, Obedience, Agility and Working Trials)

Studbook No.	Dog Name	Date	Show / Society
Breed: **Staffordshire Bull Terrier**		*Year:* **1983**	
Champion			
0520BS	GOLDWYN LUCKY STAR	27/05/1983	Bath Canine Society
Breed: **Staffordshire Bull Terrier**		*Year:* **1984**	
Champion			
3821BR	AINSAIR FANCY LASS	13/10/1984	Southern Counties Staffordshire Bull Terrier
1789BS	ALLENDALE KING	17/07/1984	East Of England Agricultural Society
5281BS	BELLE HURRICANE DUCHESS	29/09/1984	Belfast Dog Show Society
1526BT	BELNITE BELLADONNA	23/09/1984	Pyrenean Mountain Dog Club Of Scotland
1787BS	BEN HUR	12/06/1984	Three Counties Agricultural Society
0725BS	CARNDEARG JAKE THE RAKE	04/05/1984	Birmingham Dog Show Society Ltd
3420BS	ECCSTAFF TUXEDO WARRIOR	04/11/1984	Staffordshire Bull Terrier Club
0817BR	LYDES HERMIONE	27/08/1984	Leicester City Canine Society
2912BR	SCARTHWAITE REMA	07/07/1984	South Wales Kennel Association
3900BR	TEUTONIC WARRIOR	29/09/1984	Belfast Dog Show Society
1901BP	TRIDWR DICEY RILEY	07/07/1984	South Wales Kennel Association

Breed: Staffordshire Bull Terrier   **Year: 1985**

Champion

4071BT	BELNITE BLITZKRIEG	26/05/1985	Staffordshire Bull Terrier Club
4176BT	BOLDMORE BLACK SABBATH	24/10/1985	Midland Counties Canine Society
1128BT	CONTESSA OF ELVINOR	17/05/1985	Scottish Kennel Club
4144BT	CRADBURY FLASH BOYO	05/07/1985	Windsor Dog Show Society
0316BU	EASTAFF GUARDIAN	01/06/1985	Southern Counties Canine Association
1959BT	HOPLITE ANOTHER ACE	03/03/1985	Yorkshire Welsh Corgi Club
1962BT	KARJOBRI PURE SILK	25/04/1985	West Of England Ladies Kennel Society
0271BU	MUD GUTS	03/03/1985	Yorkshire Welsh Corgi Club
4282BT	RENDORN DRUMMER BOY OF KAZEMICK	05/10/1985	Western Staffordshire Bull Terrier Society
2615BU	SNOW QUEEN	13/12/1985	Ladies Kennel Association
1524BT	SPADILLE MIDNIGHT LACE	08/02/1985	Crufts
4012BT	TONDOO MISS MOON SHINE	28/06/1985	South Wales Kennel Association
2423BU	TOPCROFT TRAILBLAZER	22/09/1985	Northern Counties Staffordshire Bull Terrier

Breed: Staffordshire Bull Terrier   **Year: 1986**

Champion

3217BT	CARAVELLA QUEEN	05/04/1986	National Terrier Club
4145BT	DEVIL'S TRILL	11/07/1986	South Wales Kennel Association
4220BT	FULFIN BLACK EAGLE	29/08/1986	City Of Birmingham Canine Association
1527BT	HAMASON RED REKNOWN	14/06/1986	Border Union Agricultural Society
4235BT	JACMARTYN JACKS JEWEL	22/06/1986	Blackpool & District Canine Society

Breed: Staffordshire Bull Terrier

Champion

4858BU	JENABECK GWENLLIAN	09/06/1986	Three Counties Agricultural Society
4857BU	LAWBURY CRACKLING ROSE	05/10/1986	North Eastern Staffordshire Bull Terrier Club
4172BT	LAWBURY SPIKER JOE	22/06/1986	Blackpool & District Canine Society
4716BU	MAD MAX OF HAZELDEAN	10/05/1986	Scottish Staffordshire Bull Terrier Club
1509BV	RENDORN RIGHT MARKER	13/09/1986	Darlington Dog Show Society
4253BT	SPARTAN VICTOR	09/11/1986	East Midlands Staffordshire Bull Terrier Club
0795BV	WALLACE THE WIZARD	19/07/1986	Potteries Staffordshire Bull Terrier Club

Year: 1986

Breed: Staffordshire Bull Terrier

Champion

Year: 1987

4872BU	ASHMOSS WHITE WIZARD	28/03/1987	North West Staffordshire Bull Terrier Club
0168BW	BELNITE MARBILLUS	08/10/1987	Driffield Agricultural Society
3651BV	CHARLEMAGNE OF JUDAEL	03/10/1987	Western Staffordshire Bull Terrier Society
1470BT	CRACKERJACK OF TRIDWR	23/04/1987	West Of England Ladies Kennel Society
0222BU	DOSANTORS MOLLY MAQUIRE	10/07/1987	South Wales Kennel Association
0319BU	DUKE OF DUCKS HILL	28/03/1987	North West Staffordshire Bull Terrier Club
0687BW	EASTAFF IRONSIDES	31/08/1987	Leicester City Canine Society
3646BV	JACKSTAFF HEAVEN SENT	31/08/1987	Leicester City Canine Society
4315BW	JACKSTAFF PRIMA DONNA	15/11/1987	East Midlands Staffordshire Bull Terrier Club
1540BU	LANCSTAFF RORAS ROSIE RED	20/06/1987	Border Union Agricultural Society
3652BV	LEADING LADIES CHOICE	28/08/1987	Scottish Kennel Club

Reg No	Name	Date	Show
4903BV	LENDEVS DARK STAR OF BARNARD	09/05/1987	Scottish Staffordshire Bull Terrier Club
3094BV	MALJUE CUTTERS BOY	19/03/1987	Manchester Dog Show Society
4226BT	RECKLESS LASS	14/08/1987	Welsh Kennel Club
1552BV	RENDORN APOLLYON	01/05/1987	Birmingham Dog Show Society Ltd
3259BT	ROWENDA FEARLESS LAD	23/05/1987	Bath Canine Society
4770BU	WARCLOUD OF IRONSTONE	25/04/1987	Southern West Highland White Terrier Club
0859BS	YUILLSTAFF DARK SULTAN	26/06/1987	Blackpool & District Canine Society

Breed: Staffordshire Bull Terrier   **Year: 1988**

Champion

Reg No	Name	Date	Show
2122BW	GLYNSTAFF BORIS THE BOLD	25/02/1988	Manchester Dog Show Society
5021BS	HILLANVALE DESTINY	19/07/1988	East Of England Agricultural Society
0784BX	INDIANA ACID QUEEN ***** SEE ADD INFO *****	08/10/1988	Southern Counties Staffordshire Bull Terrier
0627BW	LANCSTAFF SPARBU SAGA	20/05/1988	Scottish Kennel Club
5024BW	MASTER JAY	23/07/1988	Leeds City & District Canine Association
2437BU	MIDDAY WONDER OF ANGELSTAFF	13/10/1988	Driffield Agricultural Society
4895BV	PRINCESS PAPILLON	18/06/1988	Border Union Agricultural Society
1511BV	RELLIM BLACK ACE	30/07/1988	Notts & Derby District Staffordshire Bull Terr
4312BW	ROCKYS BLACK SEA-EAGLE	01/10/1988	Western Staffordshire Bull Terrier Society
2121BW	SCARTHWAITE DIPLOMAT	14/05/1988	Scottish Staffordshire Bull Terrier Club
2884BW	SILVER BOMBER	28/05/1988	Bath Canine Society
1644BX	SKERRY DHU OF DUMBRITON	13/11/1988	Merseyside Staffordshire Bull Terrier Club
3261BT	SURESTAFF APHRODITE	01/07/1988	Windsor Dog Show Society

| 0347BX | ZARA THE PIED PIPER | 24/06/1988 | Blackpool & District Canine Society |
| 1936BT | ZULU WARRIOR OF ANSELMO | 01/07/1988 | Windsor Dog Show Society |

Breed: Staffordshire Bull Terrier   **Year: 1989**

Champion

1393BX	BELNITE DARK HUNTSMAN	09/02/1989	Crufts
5263BX	BLACK ICE	24/09/1989	Northern Counties Staffordshire Bull Terrier
5290BX	COAL QUEEN	20/05/1989	North Of Scotland Staffordshire Bull Terrier (
5790BX	CONSTONES YER MAN	01/05/1989	East Anglian Staffordshire Bull Terrier Club
4934BX	EASTAFF NOIRE-FILLE	19/05/1989	Scottish Kennel Club
1408BY	EDGESTAFF LUCKY LADY	25/08/1989	Scottish Kennel Club
5038BX	EILDER RED SHADOW	18/07/1989	East Of England Agricultural Society
4083BX	GRANGE SPITFIRE	02/06/1989	Southern Counties Canine Association
1364BY	JUDAEL VESTAJAY OF LINESTAFF	12/07/1989	Paignton & District Fanciers' Association
1133BW	MASTER ANTON	28/08/1989	Leicester City Canine Society
2553BW	PARKSTAFF WITCH OF THE NORTH	26/03/1989	North West Staffordshire Bull Terrier Club
3925BW	RELLIM TASK FORCE OF NOZAC	30/07/1989	Notts & Derby District Staffordshire Bull Terr
4716BW	RENDORN THE RENAGADE OF LINESTAFF	15/10/1989	North Eastern Staffordshire Bull Terrier Club
2517BX	ROCELLIO RIP VAN WINKLE	22/07/1989	Leeds City & District Canine Association
3305BX	SPARTAN WILD THYME	15/07/1989	Potteries Staffordshire Bull Terrier Club
2963BX	SPRINGSTEEN BOY	12/07/1989	Paignton & District Fanciers' Association

Breed: Staffordshire Bull Terrier   **Year: 1990**

Champion

4456BY	BONZARIES KELIBOY	14/10/1990	North Eastern Staffordshire Bull Terrier Club
1404BY	CHEWBACCA THE WOOKIE	05/07/1990	South Wales Kennel Association
3668BX	EASTAFF LIL' STOTTER	22/06/1990	Blackpool & District Canine Society
1898BZ	JACKSTAFF FORGET ME NOT	22/09/1990	Belfast Dog Show Society
1111BX	KALAHARI QUEEN	14/07/1990	Potteries Staffordshire Bull Terrier Club
5493BY	LANGROVE MALTSTER	29/07/1990	Notts & Derby District Staffordshire Bull Terr
1407BY	MAKEREADY HUNTSMAN'S LASS	15/04/1990	Staffordshire Bull Terrier Club Of South Wal
2258BY	ROGUE SAGA	11/10/1990	Driffield Agricultural Society
1677BY	TENAX CHRISTMAS STAR	24/08/1990	Scottish Kennel Club
5494BY	WAYSTAFF BOLD AS BRASS	06/09/1990	Richmond Dog Show Society

Breed: Staffordshire Bull Terrier   **Year: 1991**

Champion

3055BX	ALIDAV THE BEDFORD SQUATTER	05/09/1991	Richmond Dog Show Society
1777BZ	BATED BREATH AT CONSTONES	06/10/1991	Staffordshire Bull Terrier Club
5106BZ	BULLSEYE OF DOGAN	06/04/1991	National Terrier Club
1135BZ	CABALLERO FIRE FIGHTER	13/07/1991	Potteries Staffordshire Bull Terrier Club
1078BZ	EBONY DREADNOUGHT	25/04/1991	West Of England Ladies Kennel Society
1468CA	FROMESTAFF NETTLE OF WYREFARE	28/09/1991	Belfast Dog Show Society
5295BZ	INDIANA JET SETTER	23/08/1991	Scottish Kennel Club
2071BZ	JACKSTAFF FATAL ATRACTION	25/04/1991	West Of England Ladies Kennel Society

1580BZ	JUDAEL MAGIE NOIRE	21/06/199?	Blackpool & District Canine Society
0961CA	LETHAL WEAPON OF CRASHKON	23/08/1991	Scottish Kennel Club
1405BZ	MINTMAR MEAN MARLENE	15/06/1991	Border Union Agricultural Society
1776BZ	MISTRESS MCGRATH OF BOLDMORE	28/07/1991	Notts & Derby District Staffordshire Bull Terr
2652BZ	PARKSTAFF SPECIAL ENVOY AT JACKSTAFF	27/05/1991	East Anglian Staffordshire Bull Terrier Club
3846BY	TAKIRON DARK DISTROYER	13/12/1991	Ladies Kennel Association
3867BY	TIKKURILAN GIDDY KIPPER	16/08/1991	Welsh Kennel Club
5390BY	TOFO O'HENRY	13/10/1991	North Eastern Staffordshire Bull Terrier Club

Breed: Staffordshire Bull Terrier   **Year: 1992**

Champion

1764CA	BOLDBULL BLACK JACK	25/07/1992	Notts & Derby District Staffordshire Bull Terr
0330BZ	CLAIRWELL LADY IN RED	18/04/1992	Northern Ireland Staffordshire Bull Terrier Cl
2219BZ	ENSBURY'S LITTLE LAD AT SHIRESTAFF	12/04/1992	Staffordshire Bull Terrier Club Of South Wal
3832CA	HOT PURSUIT	07/05/1992	Birmingham Dog Show Society Ltd
4816CA	JUDAEL MASQUERADE	25/05/1992	East Anglian Staffordshire Bull Terrier Club
4522CA	KABLICE MIDNIGHT CALLER	21/07/1992	East Of England Agricultural Society
0226CB	MIDNIGHT HUNTRESS	21/07/1992	East Of England Agricultural Society
5293BZ	PITBAR REBEL WARLORD	27/09/1992	Northern Counties Staffordshire Bull Terrier
0225CB	VEE'S DREAM BOY	26/09/1992	Belfast Dog Show Society
5532CA	WHITE OF MORN	15/06/1992	Three Counties Agricultural Society
1506BZ	YORKSTAFF SILVER SAGA	23/04/1992	West Of England Ladies Kennel Society
4495CA	ZABARETTS RAZZLE DAZZLE	15/11/1992	Merseyside Staffordshire Bull Terrier Club

Breed: Staffordshire Bull Terrier **Year: 1993**

Champion

1407BZ	ALPAKA HONKY TONK WOMAN	14/01/1993	Crufts
1579BZ	ANTROBIAN DANCING BRAVE	14/06/1993	Three Counties Agricultural Society
3368CB	BEKANBAR BAROLO	14/06/1993	Three Counties Agricultural Society
4251CB	BOLDMORE FINBAR FUREY	07/11/1993	East Midlands Staffordshire Bull Terrier Club
0569CB	BOURTIE HEAT SEEKER	28/03/1993	North West Staffordshire Bull Terrier Club
1110CB	DEBRELLA TABOO DHU AT DUMBRITON	20/07/1993	East Of England Agricultural Society
0566CB	HOLMESTAFF KING ARTHUR	18/09/1993	Darlington Dog Show Society
0667CB	OCTOBER PRESIOUS GEM	08/07/1993	South Wales Kennel Association
2282CB	PANTYCELYN HAGLER	17/10/1993	North Eastern Staffordshire Bull Terrier Club
1216BY	RAMBLIX ROBERTO	03/05/1993	East Anglian Staffordshire Bull Terrier Club
1082BZ	ROWENDA DARK DESTROYER	28/05/1993	Bath Canine Society
5529CA	SHER KHAN	25/09/1993	Belfast Dog Show Society

Breed: Staffordshire Bull Terrier **Year: 1994**

Champion

1108CB	BARCUD SILVER MACHINE	20/11/1994	Staffordshire Bull Terrier Club
3140CD	BARDA THE BUSHRANGER	23/10/1994	Southern Counties Staffordshire Bull Terrier
4929CA	CRASHKON HIGH SOCIETY OF BROADWAR	17/09/1994	Darlington Dog Show Society
2477CD	DOMINO FLASHY LAD	28/04/1994	West Of England Ladies Kennel Society
0726CD	EASTSTAR ULTIMATE WARRIOR	19/07/1994	East Of England Agricultural Society
0571CB	FROMESTAFF ABRACADABRA OF WYREFARE	02/04/1994	National Terrier Club

Code	Name	Date	Organisation
2957CB	GLOWOOD RED IMAGE	18/06/1994	Border Union Agricultural Society
0729CD	JUDAEL DARK REALITY AT CAVSTAFF	20/08/1994	Staffordshire Bull Terrier Club Of South Wal
3733CB	KOOL AS ICE	24/07/1994	Notts & Derby District Staffordshire Bull Terr
3238CD	LOOK ME OVER	09/12/1994	Ladies Kennel Association
2606CD	MARY QUEEN OF STAFFS AT VULCANSTAFF	13/07/1994	Paignton & District Fanciers' Association
2806CD	QUARTERFLASH WARSQUAW	07/07/1994	South Wales Kennel Association
1124CD	SCARTHWAITE BEWITCHED	16/10/1994	North Eastern Staffordshire Bull Terrier Club
3617CB	SPARSTAFF DOMINATOR	27/05/1994	Bath Canine Society
3311CB	STAFFMASTER PURE OPIUM	18/06/1994	Border Union Agricultural Society
3180CB	STORMSTAFF SKY'S THE LIMIT	27/05/1994	Bath Canine Society
2435CE	VALGLO COROLLA	23/10/1994	Southern Counties Staffordshire Bull Terrier
0977CD	YORKSTAFF CRACKERJACK	02/04/1994	National Terrier Club

Breed: Staffordshire Bull Terrier   *Year: 1995*

Champion

Code	Name	Date	Organisation
2924CE	BEACONMOOR CHRISTMAS STAR	12/10/1995	Driffield Agricultural Society
4242CE	BELLGLEN BRAWS BEST	20/05/1995	Scottish Kennel Club
0664CE	BELLGLEN RICH DESIRE OF RIKAMIA	11/08/1995	Bournemouth Canine Association
3597CE	CROSSGUNS REVOLUTION	27/04/1995	West Of England Ladies Kennel Society
2415CF	CROSSGUNS SATURDAY SPECIAL AT BERLSCAR	07/10/1995	Western Staffordshire Bull Terrier Society
3421CB	DEBRELLA SCOTCH ON THE ROCKS OF DUMBRI	18/07/1995	East Of England Agricultural Society
0373CD	DOGAN LILY BIANCA	26/03/1995	North West Staffordshire Bull Terrier Club
1115CE	EASTAFF TREFOIL	24/09/1995	Northern Counties Staffordshire Bull Terrier

1067CF	FROMESTAFF THE MINSTREL	24/09/1995	Northern Counties Staffordshire Bull Terrier
4241CE	HAZESTAFF KEGRA RED AMBER	08/12/1995	Ladies Kennel Association
3982CD	HIGHLANDS PIED PIPER	02/06/1995	Southern Counties Canine Association
1709CA	JODEL'S BOX OF DELIGHTS	21/10/1995	Southern Counties Staffordshire Bull Terrier
1824CE	JUDAEL BOTH BARRELS AT NOZAC	15/04/1995	Northern Ireland Staffordshire Bull Terrier Cl
0723CD	KENINE DEVA-ANVIL OF AMBESTEN	21/10/1995	Southern Counties Staffordshire Bull Terrier
2637CB	NETHERTONION ROSE	26/10/1995	Midland Counties Canine Society
3139CD	NORDIC CHIEF	06/07/1995	South Wales Kennel Association
3907CE	SZONDU ULSTER MADDY	05/11/1995	East Midlands Staffordshire Bull Terrier Club

Breed: Staffordshire Bull Terrier   *Year: 1996*

Champion

0767CF	BELSEVORE ROSS-N-CO	18/05/1996	Scottish Kennel Club
4081CE	BLITSTAFF MAD O'ROURKE	30/08/1996	City Of Birmingham Canine Association
1636CF	BOMBSTAFF BLACKTHORN AT BULLHAWK	11/06/1996	Three Counties Agricultural Society
2260CF	BULLYVIEW ALRIGHT MATE	06/04/1996	National Terrier Club
1248CG	CHELMSTAFF CHRISTMAS JOY AT RAMSHIRE	03/11/1996	East Midlands Staffordshire Bull Terrier Club
2926CE	DONNELLAS GET UP AND GO	18/09/1996	Scottish Kennel Club
2810CE	EDGESTAFF TAMMY GIRL	14/03/1996	Crufts
1481CG	JAMARVINS FEMME FATALE OF VANORIC	11/10/1996	Driffield Agricultural Society
1947CE	RAMBLIX RENAISSANCE	11/06/1996	Three Counties Agricultural Society
3318CF	STORMLODGE ANNE BONNY	20/07/1996	Potteries Staffordshire Bull Terrier Club
4109CE	THE SLINGSHOT ELECTRAGLIDE	29/06/1996	Paignton & District Fanciers' Association
0623CF	TIMGOLD RITA THE RAVER	06/09/1996	Richmond Dog Show Society

Breed: Staffordshire Bull Terrier **Year: 1997**

Champion

1296CG	BRYSTAFF MINDERN ROSE AT OBMARSTAFF	06/03/1997	Crufts
2301CG	BRYSTAFF SIMPLY THE BEST	30/03/1997	North West Staffordshire Bull Terrier Club
2745CG	CANNY BAIRN FOR JAYNEZE	06/06/1997	Southern Counties Canine Association
3893CF	HIGHLAND DREAM	11/07/1997	South Wales Kennel Association
2261CF	JACKBULL JEFF'S PAL	17/05/1997	Scottish Kennel Club
3015CG	JAGSSTAFF BLACK BELIZE	05/09/1997	Richmond Dog Show Society
3642CG	RYESTAFF EBONY EYES	02/11/1997	East Midlands Staffordshire Bull Terrier Club
2186CG	SEREN'S BABY LLEUAD OF DOGAN	29/08/1997	City Of Birmingham Canine Association
1482CG	SPIRESTAFF AVENGING ANGEL OF TIKKURILAN	13/09/1997	Darlington Dog Show Society
1999CG	VALGLO LANCER	05/04/1997	National Terrier Club

Breed: Staffordshire Bull Terrier **Year: 1998**

Champion

3301CH	ARAIDH DOT TO DOT	01/11/1998	East Midlands Staffordshire Bull Terrier Club
0730CH	BARDA THE GABBA	20/06/1998	Border Union Agricultural Society
0732CH	BEEBEEMI CLAUDIUS	11/09/1998	Richmond Dog Show Society
0733CH	BETHANE MOONLIGHT MADONA	06/06/1998	Southern Counties Canine Association
1807CH	BOMBSTAFF CARLSBERG	07/05/1998	Birmingham Dog Show Society Ltd
3002CI	BOWTMAN RAZEL DAZEL	22/11/1998	Staffordshire Bull Terrier Club
1819CH	BOWTMAN'S DOUBLE TROUBLE	15/06/1998	Three Counties Agricultural Society
1658CH	FAULDSTAFF FIREFLASH	18/07/1998	Potteries Staffordshire Bull Terrier Club

Code	Name	Date	Society
1952CH	JACKSTAFF FASINATION	16/05/1998	Scottish Kennel Club
0553CI	JODEL'S MR COOL	14/08/1998	Welsh Kennel Club
1074CI	KNOCKON HOCUS POCUS	03/07/1998	Windsor Dog Show Society
1559CH	MISTLETOE MAGIC	04/04/1998	National Terrier Club
0082CG	MYESTAFF WHITE SILK	10/07/1998	South Wales Kennel Association
3350CG	RENDORN REVELATION	04/09/1998	City Of Birmingham Canine Association
2562CG	SPIRESTAFF JIMMY JAZZ	29/03/1998	North West Staffordshire Bull Terrier Club
2557CH	WYREFARE PRINCE NASEEM	18/10/1998	Southern Counties Staffordshire Bull Terrier

Breed: Staffordshire Bull Terrier   **Year: 1999**

Champion

Code	Name	Date	Society
0703CI	CONSTONES HIGH FIVE	19/06/1999	Border Union Agricultural Society
0058CI	ELVINOR PIED PRINCESS AT WAYSTAFF	24/07/1999	Leeds City & District Canine Association
3836CI	FERNSTAFF SPECIAL QUEST	24/06/1999	Blackpool & District Canine Society
4211CI	POLYNESIAN WAKA NAVIGATOR	25/09/1999	Belfast Dog Show Society
2937CH	SPARSTAFF DODGY DOCKER	21/03/1999	North West Staffordshire Bull Terrier Club
0522CJ	VANORIC VOO DOO	23/05/1999	Scottish Staffordshire Bull Terrier Club
2619CI	WINTERS MYSTIC GEM	04/06/1999	Southern Counties Canine Association

Breed: Staffordshire Bull Terrier   **Year: 2000**

Champion

Code	Name	Date	Society
1493CJ	AYMSTAFF SCARY SPICE	22/07/2000	Leeds City & District Canine Association
3405CI	BOMBADIER BILLY	20/04/2000	Birmingham Dog Show Society Ltd
1294CG	BOWTMAN'S RED OCTOBER	12/06/2000	Three Counties Agricultural Society

Code	Name	Date	Club
2181CJ	CRAGAILS BLACKEEN	25/11/2000	Staffordshire Bull Terrier Club Of South Wal
1293CG	DINALGHI DECOY	18/08/2000	Welsh Kennel Club
1395CJ	KANNECHOR YOUNG HUSTLER	09/03/2000	Crufts
2345CI	KNOCKON HALLOWEEN QUEEN	15/04/2000	Northern Ireland Staffordshire Bull Terrier Cl
1625CK	MARSTAFFS EASTER SURPRISE HOPLITE	12/08/2000	Bournemouth Canine Association
0727CH	QUEST FOR FAME	01/04/2000	National Terrier Club
2449CH	REBEL DARK ANGEL OF TRENSTAFF	15/09/2000	Darlington Dog Show Society
4008CI	SALLY'S OUR CHOICE	29/05/2000	East Anglian Staffordshire Bull Terrier Club
2847CH	SLATADY MIKE OF MENSSANA	26/10/2000	Midland Counties Canine Society
1911CI	TEARAWAY TEMPTRESS	07/10/2000	Western Staffordshire Bull Terrier Society

Breed: Staffordshire Bull Terrier   *Year: 2001*

Champion

Code	Name	Date	Club
2043CK	ARADAZIE GIRL BY BLITSTAFF	21/10/2001	Southern Counties Staffordshire Bull Terrier
2262CK	BAYSEND MYSTICAL SECRET	29/06/2001	Windsor Dog Show Society
4398CI	BUDVISOR BLITZ	31/08/2001	City Of Birmingham Canine Association
1615CK	CONSTONES JUMP FOR JOY	25/08/2001	Scottish Staffordshire Bull Terrier Club
4533CK	CRAGAILS RED MACGREGOR	11/07/2001	Paignton & District Fanciers' Association
3585CK	CUMHIL LITTLE MISCHIEF (IKC)	11/08/2001	Bournemouth Canine Association
2045CK	DARLING CARLING	16/12/2001	Staffordshire Bull Terrier Club
2061CI	DELVESWOOD THINK TWICE	11/10/2001	Driffield Agricultural Society
2179CJ	KARMEDY VOODO MAN	25/11/2001	Staffordshire Bull Terrier Club Of South Wal
0123CK	MEGABYTE BLACK BOMBER	25/10/2001	Midland Counties Canine Society
0004CK	MIMCOL TASHA YAR	07/06/2001	Bath Canine Society

Code	Name	Date	Society
1583CJ	PLYMSTAFF GABRIELA	12/04/2001	Birmingham Dog Show Society Ltd
4325CJ	RYPARK MISTY MORN OF FARHAN	22/06/2001	Blackpool & District Canine Society
4190CK	STAFFMASTER FLASHPOINT	22/09/2001	Belfast Dog Show Society
1161CJ	TIKKURILAN POISON IVY	19/05/2001	Scottish Kennel Club
2943CL	VALGLO CASANOVA AT CROSSGUNS	16/12/2001	Staffordshire Bull Terrier Club

Breed: Staffordshire Bull Terrier   **Year: 2002**

Champion

Code	Name	Date	Society
1120CL	ARAIDH DEVIL MAY CARE	08/02/2002	Manchester Dog Show Society
3062CK	ARNHEM NICE AND SPICY	21/07/2002	Staffordshire Bull Terrier Club
1815CL	BERAKA LEYLA	09/05/2002	Birmingham Dog Show Society Ltd
2438CM	CARNIG DOT CO UK	10/10/2002	Driffield Agricultural Society
1276CM	CRAGAILS BRAW WOOER	24/11/2002	Staffordshire Bull Terrier Club Of South Wal
2693CL	CRASHKON MEL BEE	24/05/2002	Bath Canine Society
2811CL	INDIANSTAFF YOUCAN DO IT (IMP BEL)	05/10/2002	Western Staffordshire Bull Terrier Society
3201CK	LADARNA BIRTHDAY BOY	08/02/2002	Manchester Dog Show Society
2347CL	MARSTAFF DRAGON LIVES ON	24/10/2002	Midland Counties Canine Society

Breed: Staffordshire Bull Terrier   **Year: 2003**

Champion

Code	Name	Date	Society
4050CM	ASHSTOCK BY JUPITER	21/09/2003	Northern Counties Staffordshire Bull Terrier

Breed: Staffordshire Bull Terrier   **Year:** 2003

Champion

1404CM	BEKANBAR BEWITCHED	26/05/2003	East Anglian Staffordshire Bull Terrier Club
1346CL	KNOCKON DANCE WITH THE DIVIL	23/05/2003	Bath Canine Society
2291CN	LACKYLE CEAL NA OLC (IKC)	27/07/2003	Notts & Derby District Staffordshire Bull Terr
0221CL	MEGABYTE BATHSHEBA	20/06/2003	Blackpool & District Canine Society
2903CM	RUMROURKE RAPIDASH	23/08/2003	Scottish Kennel Club
1889CM	TIABO ANGEL OF THE NORTH	19/10/2003	Southern Counties Staffordshire Bull Terrier
3863CL	TORNADOSTORM THE LEGACY	19/07/2003	Potteries Staffordshire Bull Terrier Club
1777CK	WOIZEL'S WISH AT DAWN WITH SHINGSSTAFF	25/04/2003	West Of England Ladies Kennel Society

GLOSSARY OF TERMS

Affix An affix, which must consist of only one word, is attached to a dog's registered name to identify it with a particular breeder or kennel. Affixes can only be granted by the Kennel Club and attract an initial fee plus an annual maintenance fee. Normally the owner of a registered affix must use it as the first word in a dog's name when he is the breeder and the last word in the name when he is not the breeder.

Brisket The breast or more specifically the area in front of the chest situated between the front legs.

Challenge Certificate Generally abbreviated as CC, this is a Kennel Club award for the best dog of each sex in the breed at championship shows where such certificates are offered.

Champion Generally abbreviated as Ch and awarded to dogs which have gained three challenge certificates under three different judges. At least one CC must have been awarded when the dog was more than twelve months of age.

Cow hocked A condition where the hocks are bent inwards, resulting in the hind feet being forced outwards. This fault generally restricts free movement.

Cryptorchid A male dog in which neither testicle has descended into the scrotum (the bag normally containing the testicles). A highly undesirable recessive trait which normally renders the dog sterile.

Dish faced A head where the muzzle angles upwards generally forming a better defined stop. In the Stafford a slight amount of dish face is required.

Down faced The opposite to dish faced. A head where the muzzle angles downwards from the stop, as in the bull terrier.

Dudley nose Nostrils lacking in pigmentation which results in a coffee coloured appearance. A Dudley nose debars a Stafford from winning any prize in the UK. The Breed Standard describes it as a pink (Dudley) nose.

Gay tail A tail which is carried above the horizontal position. The Stafford should have a low-set tail, without much curl, which may be likened to an old-fashioned pump handle.

Hocks The joints in the hind legs between the pasterns and the stifles.

Inbreeding The mating of closely related dogs, such as brother to sister, father to daughter, mother to son.

'Level' mouth Where the incisors of the bottom jaw fit closely inside the incisors of the upper jaw. More correctly, this should be described as a scissor bite.

Line breeding The mating of more distantly related dogs, such as cousins, or uncle to niece, or aunt to nephew. Also applied to the mating of dogs that show one or two common ancestors within three generations.

Monorchid A term usually applied to a male in which only one of the two testicles has descended into the scrotum. In fact, such dogs are usually unilateral cryptorchids, as the true monorchid possesses only one testicle.

Outcrossing The mating of two dogs whose pedigrees contain no common ancestry within five or more generations. Also a generic term applied to the mating of unrelated dogs.

Overshot Where the incisor teeth of the upper jaw project over and beyond those of the lower jaw.

Pastern That part of the front leg between the knee and the foot, and that part of the hind leg between the hock and the foot.

Patella The knee cap.

Pied A dog of two colours – mainly white, with area of some other colour (generally black, red or brindle in the Stafford) irregularly covering the head and body.

Roach back One which has a concave curve along the spine, particularly about the loins.

Rose ears The commonest and most desirable type of ear in the Stafford. The ear consists of a crinkle in mid-ear and a fold near its extremity.

Splay feet Flat feet, the toes spread rather too wide apart.

Stifle Corresponds to the human knee joint joining the first and second thigh bones.

Stop The depression, necessary in the Stafford, set in front of the eyes and separating the front of the skull from the beginning of the muzzle.

Undershot Where the incisor teeth of the lower jaw project beyond those of the upper jaw.

Unilateral cryptorchid A term applied to a male in which only one of the two testicles has descended into the scrotum. See Monorchid.

Withers Area between the shoulder blades where the neck adjoins the body.

INDEX
ALSO SEE *GLOSSARY*
(Preceding pages)